THE KIKKOMAN CHRONICLES

A Global Company With a Japanese Soul

RONALD E. YATES

McGraw-Hill

New York San Francisco Washington, D.C. Auckland Bogotá
Caracas Lisbon London Madrid Mexico City Milan
Montreal New Delhi San Juan Singapore
Sydney Tokyo Toronto

For Inge,
Whose devoted patience, support, and understanding were more meaningful than she may know

McGraw-Hill

A Division of The **McGraw-Hill** *Companies*

1 2 3 4 5 6 7 8 9 0 DOC/DOC 9 0 3 2 1 0 9 8

ISBN 0-07-134736-4

The sponsoring editor for this book was Jeffrey Krames, the editing supervisor was Donna Namorato, and the production supervisor was Suzanne W. B. Rapcavage. It was set in Times Roman per the IPROA design specs by Kim Sheran of the Hightstown McGraw-Hill Desktop Publishing Unit.

This book is printed on acid-free paper.

CONTENTS

PREFACE

As with many Americans, my first encounter with the Kikkoman Corporation and its products came in a Chinese restaurant. It was a small, rather ascetic place tucked away in a back street of Boston. The dining room was rectangular in shape, maybe 40 ft long and 25 ft wide. In it were a dozen or so tables covered with gold plastic tablecloths. Each table was adorned with a small red hurricane lamp, an ashtray, and an assortment of small white porcelain bottles filled with various fluids. A red and gold plastic dragon was hung along the length of one wall. On the other wall were some faded ink drawings of Chinese mountains whose peaks were shrouded in mist. Near the restaurant's entrance was a large tank of live Maine lobsters flanked by two multicolored ginger jars.

The year was 1963, but I can still remember the interior of the restaurant because, as it turned out, it became one of my favorite Boston haunts. The restaurant, which is long since gone, was called the Red Dragon Inn. Along with a handful of army buddies, I had ducked inside the place quite by accident in order to get out of a torrential early spring rain. We had come to Boston from Ft. Devens, some 50 mi away, where we were going to school for the U.S. Army Security Agency.

Ft. Devens was located near the town of Ayer, and as far as I could tell, there wasn't a Chinese or Japanese restaurant anywhere within 50 mi of the main gate. Even in Boston in the early 1960s, Chinese restaurants were few and far between. I don't recall ever seeing a Japanese restaurant anywhere in Massachusetts in those days.

So there we were, four or five of us, all from places like Kansas, Iowa, Missouri, and Nebraska. Chinese restaurants—or any restaurant featuring food from the Orient—were about as common in our rural communities as subways or moonrocks. If any of us had ever been in a real Chinese restaurant before, it was probably because we had missed a turn on the way to the local barbecue joint or burger barn.

We hung up our soaked jackets and settled at a table along a wall under the glaring plastic dragon. After looking at the menu, we all ordered the only Chinese dishes any of us cornfed midwesterners had ever heard of: chow mein, chop suey, and sweet and sour pork.

The owner, a balding, bespectacled man in his midsixties named Mr. Choo, was moving from table to table with a 1-gal can of some dark and mysterious fluid. At each table, he deftly poured the liquid from the large can into small white porcelain bottles. Finally, Mr. Choo arrived at our table. His face was broad and round and friendly with a forehead that didn't stop until midway to the top of his head. He smiled at us, removed a porcelain stopper from one of the small bottles on our table, and proceeded to pour the inky liquid into it.

"What's that stuff?" someone asked.

"What? This?" Mr. Choo responded incredulously. "This soy sauce!"

"Soy sauce?" said a fellow named Parks who hailed from eastern Iowa where, along with Illinois, most of this nation's soybeans are grown. "Is it made from soybeans?"

"Sure, you bet," said Mr. Choo. "Soybeans and wheat."

"Wheat?" I asked. I was the one from Kansas, which just happens to grow most of America's winter wheat.

"Yep, you bet. Wheat, too," Mr. Choo laughed. "You boys not know about soy sauce, eh? Very important for Chinese food . . . Japanese food . . . all Oriental food. This number one soy sauce in whole world," he said proudly thumping the large metal can with his finger. On the can was the word "Kikkoman." It was the first time I had ever seen that name. But it wouldn't be the last.

When our food arrived, we quickly drowned it in soy sauce—figuring it was the polite thing to do. But actually, it was the wrong thing to do. Soy sauce, Mr. Choo quickly informed us, is not meant to overpower food, but to bring out its inherent flavor and taste.

"No, no. Just using a little bit please," Mr. Choo gently scolded.

Mr. Choo, who had come to the United States from the Chinese mainland in 1947 as the Chinese Nationalists of Chiang Kai-Shek and the Communists under Mao Tse-Tung (Mao Zedong) were still battling for control of the country, scurried back to the kitchen and barked out something in Cantonese. Then he came back to our table and quickly picked up our plates, which were by now engulfed in soy sauce. He sighed heavily as he looked at the food that floated in miniature lakes of amber liquid.

"Tsk, tsk," he said. "These no good now."

It turned out that Mr. Choo had ordered another large plate of Chinese dishes (on the house, no less!) including something called "pot stickers" that none of us had ever seen before. He then proceeded to show us how to use soy sauce.

"Just pouring a little out like this," he said, depositing a few drops on a lightly browned pot sticker. "That's the secret."

I felt like a student in a college chemistry class as I watched "Professor" Choo show us the proper use of soy sauce.

"Now you know the secret, too," Mr. Choo said. "Good soy sauce like good shoes. Go long, long way."

Many years later, during my first posting to Japan as Tokyo bureau chief for the *Chicago Tribune*, I learned a lot more about soy sauce. I learned, for example, that Japanese food is never served without it. In fact, Japanese cuisine is almost structured around soy sauce. And I learned something about the Kikkoman Corporation, too. I learned that between 1972 and 1973—a year before I was posted to Japan by the *Chicago Tribune*—it had opened a soy sauce plant in Walworth, Wisconsin. I had no idea where Walworth was, nor did I know at the time that it was the first significant Japanese manufacturing facility ever built in the United States.

What I did know is that I could not eat Chinese or Japanese food without soy sauce. And even though I couldn't tell you why in those days, I also knew that Kikkoman Soy Sauce was head and shoulders above all others. But it wasn't until I met Kikkoman president and CEO Yuzaburo Mogi during a meeting of the Japan-Midwest Society in Milwaukee, Wisconsin, in 1991 that I finally learned why I liked Kikkoman better than any other soy sauce I could buy from my local supermarket.

"Our soy sauce is naturally brewed," Mogi said. He explained that it takes several months to produce Japanese-style *shoyu,* or soy sauce, and that one of the secrets to its distinctive and complex taste lies in the addition of wheat during the long fermentation process.

After talking with Mogi about Kikkoman, soy sauce, the company's incredible 360-plus-year history, and its success at fitting into a small farming community like Walworth with a totally alien product, I decided that this was a company ripe for a cover story in the *Chicago Tribune* Sunday Magazine.

The response to the article was amazing. Only a cover story I had done on W. Edwards Deming—America's so-called "curmudgeon of quality"—elicited more mail. Not only did people know about Kikkoman Soy Sauce, many were familiar with the company and its long history in the United States.

"How refreshing," one reader wrote in a letter to me in January 1993." A Japanese company that seems to be doing everything right at a time when U.S. Congressmen are smashing Japanese cars and electronic products with sledge hammers in Washington. Can this kind of success rub off on the rest of us?"

I don't know if that's a question this book can answer. But I do know the reason I wrote it. During my career as a journalist, I have researched and written about some of the world's most respected and benchmarked companies: Motorola, Inc.; Honda Motor Co. Ltd; Eastman Kodak Co.; Sony Corp.; FMC Corp.; Microsoft Corp.; to name a few. Kikkoman Corporation may not be in the same league as these companies when it comes to sales or the size of its bottom line. But when it comes to creative energy, innovative and aggressive marketing, or the treatment of employees, suppliers, and customers, Kikkoman belongs right there at the top of the list. What's more, despite its more than 300 years of recorded history, the Kikkoman Corporation may be one of Japan's (and the world's) best kept secrets. With this book, the secret is out. Or as Mr. Choo, my first "professor" of soy sauce, would no doubt say: "Now you know the secret, too."

INTRODUCTION

Most people know the Kikkoman Corporation as a producer of soy sauce. And why not? Bottles of the company's products are a fixture in 25 percent of America's restaurants and 99 percent of its supermarkets. With their red caps, their hexagonal logo, and their yellow, black, red, white, and blue labels, bottles of Kikkoman's ebony flavor-enhancing seasoning are among the most distinctive products in the world.

But it's what people don't know about Kikkoman that is most intriguing. For example, few people are aware that Kikkoman was the first Japanese company to set up a full-blown manufacturing facility in the United States. At the same time, few people outside of Japan know that Kikkoman is one of the oldest continuously operated enterprises among Japan's largest manufacturing companies. Its roots can be traced back to 1630—about the same time that Japan's rigid and autocratic Tokugawa Shogunate was beginning. The Tokugawa Shogunate was a 265-year span of feudalism that began in 1603, when Japan shut its doors to the outside world and didn't end until forced to do so in 1868 when the Emperor Meiji wrested power away from the ruling shogun. But unlike the Tokugawa shoguns, who didn't survive Japan's entry into the twentieth century, Kikkoman is still being led by the descendants of its founder—a span of more than 300 years. That kind of longevity shouldn't surprise those familiar with the Kikkoman logo, which was registered with the central Japanese government as an official brand name in 1838.

The word *Kikkoman* is a combination of three Japanese characters: "ki," meaning tortoise; "ko," meaning first-rate; and "man," meaning 10,000 years or forever. At the same time, the Japanese word *kikko* means hexagon, or six-sided. According to Japanese folklore, a tortoise is the symbol for long life and good fortune. A close look at the logo found on Kikkoman products reveals a hexagonal tortoise shell. Inside the shell is the Chinese character for 10,000. Thus, a literal interpretation of the Kikkoman name might be something like: A top-quality product made by a first-rate company that will live forever.

And here is a unique twist in a country where business has been traditionally dominated by men: Kikkoman, one of Japan's oldest companies, was founded by a woman. Her family name was Maki. She was the maternal ancestor of Yuzaburo Mogi, the U.S.-educated CEO who runs Kikkoman today. He remembers his father referring to her as Shige (pronounced *She-gay*) Maki. How many companies anywhere can claim those kind of bloodlines?

It was not surprising that Shige Maki founded one of Japan's oldest companies. After all, this was a strong and audacious woman with a keen sense of survival. As it turned out, she would need all three attributes.

Japan in the early seventeenth century was a land at war with itself. Powerful warlords vying for control of the countryside waged bloody and seemingly constant battles with one another. Vast armies of samurai warriors swept over the country laying siege to castles and cities. It was in this climate that Shige Maki found herself living in Osaka Castle where her husband was a samurai warrior serving the warlord Toyotomi Hideyori.

Toyotomi was a bitter rival of Tokugawa Ieyasu—the first of Japan's powerful line of Tokugawa shoguns who would rule Japan virtually unchallenged until the mid-nineteenth century when Commodore Matthew Perry and his squadron of black ships forced Japan to open its doors to global politics and commerce.

But in the early 1600s, the first Tokugawa shogun was still trying to consolidate his power through a campaign of political and military intimidation. It was this goal that brought Tokugawa's army to the foot of Osaka Castle in 1615. Toyotomi was in no mood to be intimidated by Tokugawa or any other rival warlord, and he told Tokugawa so. Nevertheless, Tokugawa laid siege to the castle, and in the bloody battle that followed, Shige Maki's husband died along with Toyotomi and his entire family.

Shige Maki and her son would have been put to the sword, too, had she not kept her wits. She and her son slipped away during the chaos and carnage of battle and, disguised as peasants, made their way 300 mi up country to an area just north of Edo (today's Tokyo). There, they settled in the village of Noda. Because Shige Maki and all others who had supported Toyotomi were on Tokugawa Ieyasu's death list, she changed her name to Mogi and blended in with the rice farmers in the area. For 15 years, she and her son cultivated rice and in the process learned the craft of brewing *shoyu*—the Japanese word for soy sauce.

Two earlier, more primitive forerunners of the condiment called *jiang* and *chi* (soy nuggets) are mentioned in Chinese literature dating back to 300 B.C., according to research by the Soyfoods Center in Lafayette, California. Both had been used for centuries as a way to preserve meat and fish over the winter. *Hishio*, the earliest known ancestor of modern soy sauce, was introduced to Japan in the seventh or eighth century—about 1000 years before Shige Maki began making her shoyu.

Using her new name of Mogi, the resourceful woman who narrowly escaped the swords of Tokugawa's army made some refinements to the production process and more than 300 years ago began making the product that the world today knows as Kikkoman.

Kikkoman's history is one that few, if any, of the world's corporations can match. With that kind of pedigree, one might assume that Kikkoman would be a conservative company steeped in tradition. Although Kikkoman does indeed honor its traditions (it maintains, after all, a small traditional plant where it brews soy sauce specially for Japan's imperial family), it is not mired in them.

The story of the 300-year-old Kikkoman Corporation is a story about how one of Japan's most traditional enterprises has combined modern technology with ancient craftsmanship and skill to expand production of what is generally regarded as humankind's oldest condiment (soy sauce) and sell it in about 100 countries along with an impressive array of 2000 other products.

It's an expansion that includes the opening in Walworth, Wisconsin, of the largest soy sauce plant in the Western world. As a result of that move, consumption of soy sauce in the United States alone has increased tenfold during the past 20 years and demand in Europe is rising dramatically.

Why the growing popularity of soy sauce in the West? First, soy sauce possesses the unique ability to enhance rather than overpower a wide assortment of international dishes. Second, Kikkoman has employed a daring, compelling, and innovative management style and marketing strategy that other Japanese companies consistently benchmark. The company first began prime time television advertising of its soy sauce in the United States during the 1956 presidential election returns. That was a full year before Americans saw TV ads for the Toyopet, the first car Toyota sold in the United States.

Of course, marketing strategies are only as good as a company's products and services. Where Kikkoman has really demonstrated leadership and originality is in its aggressive use of science and technology to improve and broaden its product line. Kikkoman is still the world's largest soy sauce manufacturer, with 30 percent of the Japanese market. Soy sauce remains its core product but the company is also a leader in using genetic engineering, biotechnology, and biochemistry to create a broad range of new products that are far removed from soy sauce. For example, using cell-fusion technology, Kikkoman has developed an entirely new species of citrus plant. It has even found a use for the humble firefly—an insect mentioned often in Japanese literature and folklore. Using recombinant DNA technology, Kikkoman is producing firefly luciferase, a bioluminescent enzyme used to test food for unwanted microorganisms such as the dreaded E. *coli*.

This kind of resourcefulness and initiative is not new at Kikkoman. It has been one of the constant drivers of the company as it has gone from one of Japan's most traditional domestic companies to one of its most daring global corporations.

Back in the early 1970s, when Japanese companies like Toyota and Sony were still only thinking about setting up manufacturing facilities in the United States, Kikkoman had already done it. It was Kikkoman—not Toyota or Sony or Matsushita—that was the first Japanese company to construct and operate a full-blown manufacturing facility in the United States. That occurred with little fanfare between 1972 and 1973—more than 10 years before the first Toyota rolled off an American assembly line. The site was Walworth, Wisconsin—a small farming community in the middle of the Big Foot Prairie of southern Wisconsin. While most Americans knew what a Japanese-made Toyota looked like, you could count on one hand the number of people in this stronghold of traditional food groups who could tell the difference between soy sauce and India ink.

How times have changed. Today, soy sauce has become Wisconsin's "other" brew. And the Kikkoman plant on the outskirts of the little town of Walworth (pop. 1600) is one of Kikkoman's most productive. Even more remarkable is how Kikkoman has managed to blend into a rural Wisconsin community. Kikkoman's success in Walworth is no accident. It is part of a well-orchestrated corporate policy designed to integrate Kikkoman's Japanese managers and employees with the local community.

If this strategy sounds familiar, it is. Remember Shige Maki and her escape from the shogun? She had a knack for blending in. It's the same with Kikkoman's Japanese managers and other Japanese employees. They are required to live separately from one another in different communities rather than together in an ex-pat "Japanese ghetto." It's a strategy that eliminates suspicion, while creating a strong bond between Kikkoman's Japanese employees and their American neighbors. The company has followed the same policy in places like Singapore, Hawaii, Canada, Germany, Hong Kong, Taiwan, and Australia.

Part of Kikkoman's success at fitting in here in the United States may also have something to do with the company's product. Unlike Japanese automakers, whose products are often characterized as a "threat" or part of an "invasion," Kikkoman's assortment of soy sauces and other condiments, such as its teriyaki sauce and marinades, are nonthreatening additions to the family dinner table. Unlike Japanese automobiles, which exploded on the American scene following the 1973 oil crisis, Kikkoman's products experienced a slow and untroubled acceptance.

In the 1960s, continual study and monitoring of U.S. eating habits had convinced Kikkoman planners that a shift was under way in American homes and restaurants. Up until World War II, the main consumers of Kikkoman products in the United States were Asians and Asian Americans who were already familiar with Asian cuisine. (The company even shipped a barrel of soy sauce to Japanese Americans who were interned at Manzanar in California during World War II.) But during the postwar years, Kikkoman discovered something new about American eating habits. Non-Asian Americans were consuming the cuisine of nations such as Japan, China, Korea, and Thailand as never before. The reason? American men and women who had served in Asia during World War II, the occupation of Japan, and the Korean War had discovered Asian cuisine.

While most of this Chinese, Japanese, and Korean food was being consumed in restaurants in the 1950s and 1960s, Kikkoman research showed that Americans were nevertheless shifting toward lighter foods that could be prepared more quickly in the home. In either case, it meant that demand for soy sauce could only increase.

Kikkoman could meet that demand by ratcheting up its exports of bulk soy sauce from Japan to an American bottling company in Oakland, California. But transporting raw materials (soybeans and wheat) to Japan and then transporting the finished product back to the United States was grossly inefficient—especially at a time when U.S. consumption was rising 10 percent per year. According to Yuzaburo Mogi, moving soybeans and wheat to Japan represented a sizable investment in preproduction costs. At the same time, the cost of transporting brewed soy sauce from Japan to the United States was an equally expensive and inefficient proposition. Despite these inefficiencies, by 1971 Kikkoman had surpassed Chun King in U.S. supermarket sales of soy sauce, becoming number two behind La Choy.

If Kikkoman could be that successful exporting its product to the United States, what would happen if it began making its products in the United States? It was a question that consumed Yuzaburo Mogi, the man who today is Kikkoman's chief executive. Back then, as head of Kikkoman's planning department, Mogi had no trouble seeing the advantages of a U.S. operation.

Mogi was the first Japanese to receive an MBA from Columbia University in New York, and he had a keen understanding of the American marketplace. He had spent his college years as a part-time "demonstrator" of Kikkoman products in New York area supermarkets, urging customers to try small pieces of teriyaki (broiled meat marinated in a mixture of soy sauce, sugar, and sweet rice wine). He had seen the way Americans responded to teriyaki and other Japanese dishes and he saw opportunity.

But there was resistance within Kikkoman. A U.S. plant would be expensive. (Back in the early 1970s, it took 360 yen to buy $1, not the 115 yen or so it took in the 1990s.) And there was no guarantee that a market would develop for the soy sauce a U.S. plant would produce. As is typical in a Japanese corporation, Mogi conducted years of *nemawashi* (a Japanese word meaning "root tending") in an effort to build up support for his idea. Eventually, he prevailed, and in 1973, the Walworth plant was opened. By 1983, Kikkoman had surpassed La Choy, its number one competitor, as America's number one soy sauce maker.

That success is not simply a matter of localizing production, however. It is also a function of quality and a unique process that competitors have been unable to duplicate. Unlike American-made soy sauce, which is chemically produced within a matter of hours, Kikkoman Soy Sauce is brewed and fermented—a complex process dating back to the seventeenth century that uses a proprietary microorganism to create a culture called *koji* which is added to huge fermentation tanks filled with a brine mixture of soybeans and wheat. There it remains for several months. Eventually, a fermented semiliquid reddish-brown mash called *moromi* is created. The raw soy sauce is separated from this mixture by pressing it through layers of filtration cloth. The liquid that emerges from this process is eventually refined, pasteurized, and packaged as finished soy sauce.

Today, sales of Kikkoman Soy Sauce in overseas markets account for 26 percent of the company's $2 billion in revenues, and the company's overseas production capacity has increased eightfold.

In April 1996, Kikkoman broke ground for its first plant in Europe. It's somehow fitting that this plant is in the Netherlands. It was Dutch traders, after all, who first brought soy sauce from Japan to Europe in the early seventeenth century. The soy sauce those Dutch traders brought from Japan quickly became a "secret ingredient" used by European chefs in haute cuisine from Paris to Vienna. Kikkoman opened its new plant in the Netherlands in the fall of 1997 and it will open its second American plant in Folsom, California, in 1998.

It's been a long journey from the ashes of Osaka Castle. But as those who read this book will learn, the journey is far from over.

ACKNOWLEDGMENTS

You cannot write a book about any company without a lot of inside help. In the case of this book that help was considerable. I received crucial support, guidance and background from many people who are part of the Kikkoman "family."

First, I am grateful to Bernie Krisher, a former colleague in the Tokyo press corps and most recently, publisher and humanitarian, who brought this project to me. I also am indebted to my editor at McGraw-Hill, Jeffrey Krames, whose professionalism and advice helped make this project a joy.

Within Kikkoman I am grateful to Pat Killen, executive communications consultant, who played the important role of facilitator and *nakodo* as this book took shape between Chicago and Tokyo. Pat's quiet counsel and guidance as a member of Kikkoman's International Operations Division were invaluable. I am also indebted to Fumihide Saito, manager, Office of the President and to Julie Doerr, also of the Office of the President for their assistance in arranging interviews and facilitating my movement between Kikkoman's various plants and facilities in Japan.

I also appreciate the assistance and support provided by Mitsuo Someya, Director of Kikkoman's First International Operations Division in Tokyo. Mr. Someya did an admirable job of walking the ticklish tightrope between Kikkoman and me regarding content and style. I also want to thank the two men with the same name: Kenzaburo Mogi, Kikkoman's Executive Managing Director and Kenzaburo Mogi, Director of Kikkoman's Marketing Unit for the invaluable insights they provided.

Others in Kikkoman's various Japan-based offices and plants who provided inestimable assistance were Kaichiro Someya, director of the Office of the President; Yoshiyuki Nogi, general manager, Overseas Trade Department; Masahiro Miyashita, general manager, Foreign Procurement Department; Shinichi Jimbo, manager, public relations, Foreign Operations Department; Katsumi Ishizuka, deputy general manager, Biochemical Division; Tadao Hirayama, manager, Public Relations Department; Dr. Shigetaka

Ishii, director, Research and Development Division; Dr. Eiichi Nakano, vice director, Research and Development Division; Dr. Takanobu Nakadai, general manager, R&D Division; and Noriaki Hattori and Toshifumi Ohgawara, both of the R&D Division.

I am likewise grateful to Asao Kawamura, Corporate Auditor of the Kikkoman Corporation. Within Nippon Del Monte Corporation, I received valuable assistance from Dr. Shinichi Sugiyama, President; Saburo Kojima, Director, Production Division; and Shuji Shinohara, Corporate Strategy General Manager. In Nippon Del Monte's Numata R&D Division, I am indebted to Dr. Katsumi Yuasa, Director; Dr. Haruki Sayama and Eiji Ishimura, Senior Researchers.

In San Francisco, I want to thank Masaki Miki, President of Kikkoman International, Inc. and Kazuo Takei, senior Vice-President and National Sales Manager of Kikkoman International, Inc.

In Walworth, I received extensive support from Milton E. Neshek, General Counsel and Director of Kikkoman Foods, Inc. and Dr. Kazuya Hayashi, Executive Vice-President General Manager Kikkoman Foods, Inc.; and William F. Wythe, communications assistant for Kikkoman Foods, Inc. I also received valuable insights into Kikkoman's culture from Malcolm W. Pennington in New York. Pennington, who is a member of the Board of Directors of Kikkoman Foods, Inc., provided important historical perspective to Kikkoman's early efforts in the United States. Special thanks go to Ken Saito, who as a member of Kikkoman's International Marketing division in Oak Brook, Illinois, was instrumental in helping me do the original Chicago Tribune Sunday Magazine story on Kikkoman in 1993 and who is now a member of Kikkoman's domestic sales team in Japan.

To those I may have inadvertently left off this list, I apologize.

Finally, I want to thank Yuzaburo Mogi, president and CEO of Kikkoman Corporation for his time and insight in helping me to understand the complexities of Kikkoman's past as well as its vision of the future.

1 CHAPTER

Completing the Circle

On a crisp April day in 1996, a white-robed Shinto priest walked to a small altar draped with blue and white curtains, clapped his hands twice, and slowly intoned the Japanese words used to activate a Shinto purification ceremony. The location of this ancient ritual was not a shrine somewhere in Japan, but inside a large seven-sided tent in the town of Hoogezand-Sappemeer, the Netherlands.

More than 300 years after Dutch traders carried the first ceramic canisters of Japanese-made *shoyu* (soy sauce) to Europe, Japan's oldest and largest shoyu maker had come to the Netherlands to break ground for its first European factory, which was up and running in the autumn of 1997. As it had done 23 years earlier when it opened its first plant in the United States, the Kikkoman Corporation had engaged a Shinto priest to make sure the gods were happy with the site. Kikkoman was leaving nothing to chance.

While the decision to locate in the northern Dutch city of Hoogezand-Sappemeer was not some sentimental gesture to chronological symmetry, its historical significance nevertheless was not lost on the scores of guests who crowded into the tent. Neither was the fact that the Shinto priest was a Dutchman named Paul de Leeuw from the Netherlands's Yamakage Shinto Shrine.

In a way, it was as if the Dutch and the Japanese were completing a circle begun 328 years earlier. In the Dutch language archives of The Hague are records showing that between 1668 and 1699 a group of 16 Japanese merchants shipped large quantities of soy sauce from Japan to the Coromandel Coast in southeast India, Ceylon, Vietnam, and the Netherlands. One surviving ship manifest reveals that 12 barrels of "Japanischzoya" were shipped from Dejima in Nagasaki harbor in 1688 and "thence to Rotterdam." From the Netherlands, soy sauce apparently made its way into many of Europe's royal kitchens.

Surviving anecdotal material says that King Louis XIV, who ruled France from 1661 to 1715, considered Japanese shoyu his favorite seasoning in the royal kitchens. We may never know just how accurate that material is, but one thing is sure: Demand for soy sauce in the common kitchens of twentieth-century Europe is growing.

Which brings us back to Hoogezand-Sappemeer and an obscure Shinto ceremony under way inside a tent.

"Shubatsu-no-gi," chanted the Shinto priest, signaling the first of nine steps of the "Ji Chin Sai" meant to purify the grounds and make them ready for construction. That was followed by the "Koshin-no-gi" (descent of the deity), the "Kensen-no-gi" (offering presentation), and the "Oharai-no-gi" (the purification of the site). Finally, the priest turned and intoned: "Tamagushi Hoten," which signaled the beginning of the sacred sprig offering—the most meaningful moment in the ceremony.

Kikkoman President and Chief Executive Officer Yuzaburo Mogi stood and walked to the *saidan,* or altar. After arriving, he bowed once, extended his right hand with the palm facedown, and accepted a short sprig from the priest. With his left hand raised slightly above the right one, Mogi held the leafy end of the sprig, faced the altar, and raised the sprig to cheek level. As he faced the altar, he bowed once more, pulled his right hand with palm upward toward his body, and extended his left hand. Then he pulled his left hand toward his right hand until he could switch the leafy end of the sprig from his left to his right palm. Holding the bare end of the sprig with his left hand, he slowly turned it clockwise and then placed it gently on the altar. Mogi bowed twice, clapped his hands twice, and bowed deeply once again. He then stepped backward until he passed under a rope made of rice plants, bowed once more, and returned to his seat.

The mostly Dutch audience, which included the mayor of Hoogezand-Sappemeer and a handful of other special guests, was entranced by the ceremony.

"I have never seen a ritual so precise and yet so unpretentious," one of the guests whispered. "It seems so earthy."

The Dutch guest was very observant. The essence of the Ji Chin Sai, like all Shinto ceremonies, lies in the reverence paid to all things in nature. Japan's 2000-year-old indigenous religion, which literally means "the way of the gods," teaches that all things, both animate and inanimate, have their own *kami,* or spirits—even the ground upon which the new Kikkoman plant would be constructed.

Mogi's participation had taken all of 3 minutes, but the symbolism of the ceremony spanned centuries of Japanese history and culture. By purifying the ground upon which the plant would be built, Mogi and Kikkoman were appeasing whatever god or gods resided in the area, thus ensuring that no spiritual ill will or mischief would befall the project. After Mogi had returned to his seat, the Shinto priest removed the offerings from the altar and ended the 20-minute religious ceremony by sipping sake from a small porcelain cup.

Later, Mogi and Mrs. Anneke van Dok-van Weele, the Dutch minister of foreign trade, broke ground for the plant that will have an initial capacity of 4000 kL per year—the equivalent of 30 million small bottles of soy sauce. Eventually, the plant will turn out 30,000 kL—enough to supply every market in Europe. For Yuzaburo Mogi, the ceremony represented the culmination of a vision that he has long fostered for the Kikkoman Corporation.

"Today is a very special day for Kikkoman Corporation," Mogi told those gathered under the tent for the ceremony. "This ceremony symbolizes the start of construction at our first European production site. It means that in less than 2 years we will truly be global producers of soy sauce.

"Beginning in late 1997, Kikkoman's proprietary, fully automated brewing process will be in operation in key areas of Europe, Asia, and America," he continued. "This drive for globalization started in 1972 with the construction of our first plant outside Japan in Walworth, Wisconsin. Our second overseas plant was constructed in Singapore in 1983.

"For more than three centuries, our soy sauce has been known to Europeans," Mogi said. "It was your ancestors, the Dutch merchants, who brought soy sauce to the French court and elsewhere in Europe. Our challenge now is to make our seasoning products a common feature in European kitchens everywhere."

It was a short, typically concise speech. But it spoke volumes about Kikkoman's long-range strategic intent. An ancient condiment that has its origins during China's Chou Dynasty (1100–256 B.C.) and which found its way to Japan sometime during the seventh or eighth century would be mass produced for the first time on the European continent. The strategic thinking behind this move was the same as that which convinced Kikkoman to open its Walworth, Wisconsin, plant: By marketing soy sauce as an international "all-purpose seasoning" rather than a condiment used strictly in Oriental cooking, new markets could be developed.

It's a strategy that has paid off. Kikkoman products, which are manufactured in 12 facilities in Japan and one each in the United States, Singapore, Taiwan, and now the Netherlands can be found in about 100 countries today. Even though Kikkoman doubled its share of the Japanese market from 14 to 30 percent between 1952 and 1993, by the 1960s, domestic demand for soy sauce had flattened and was even in decline. New markets would have to be found, and even created, if Kikkoman was to remain a viable enterprise.

As far back as 1965, Kikkoman, under the leadership of Kikkoman President Keizaburo Mogi (Yuzaburo Mogi's father), began to explore the possibility of opening a manufacturing facility in the United States. For one thing, it would be cheaper than transporting raw materials (wheat and soybeans) to Japan and then shipping them back again in the form of soy sauce. There were also the vagaries of import-export regulations, which are always subject to change.

In the early 1970s, Kikkoman launched what has become a signature marketing strategy in Europe. It opened a chain of six Japanese teppanyaki steak houses in Germany. Under the name Kikkoman-Daitokai GmbH, the Düsseldorf-based Kikkoman subsidiary has successfully introduced soy sauce and traditional Japanese cuisine to hundreds of thousands of Europeans. Another subsidiary, Kikkoman Trading Europe GmbH, also based in Düsseldorf, is Kikkoman's marketing arm in Europe. Bringing consumers into restaurants allows them to try new and native cuisine prepared with things like teriyaki and sukiyaki marinades, tempura mix, stir-fry sauce, teriyaki basting glaze, and sweet and sour sauce.

The European and American marketing and manufacturing ventures were part of a three-pronged strategy designed to create new markets for soy sauce, diversify into other product areas, and expand Kikkoman's activities outside of Japan. In 1987, two more elements were added to that strategy. First, Kikkoman made an effort to adapt more quickly to evolving consumer preferences. Then it used its lineup of some 2000 different products to provide its customers with new ways to enjoy eating.

The secret to this process is finding what Kikkoman executives call "adventurous consumers"—consumers willing to try new foods or even native foods prepared differently. For the past two decades, Kikkoman marketing research has found that the most adventurous consumers in the world reside in the United States, Australia, Germany, the Netherlands, and Scandinavia. But as national borders are blurred by the increasingly rapid flow of information and technology from one end of the global economy to another, the movement of cuisine between cultures has also escalated. The result is a growing population of international consumers from China to Chile eager to experience unfamiliar dishes and flavors.

This view is not simply some marketing report's projection. It is based on fact. For example, from the time Kikkoman Soy Sauce was first exported and sold in the United States as far back as 1903, according to California's Soyfoods Center, the market was primarily Asians or Asian Americans who used it in their native cooking. But that began to change in the 1950s as more and more non-Asian-American soldiers and businesspeople returned from tours of duty in Japan and other parts of Asia. Life in Asia had taught them about Asian cuisine and the significance of soy sauce in it. At the same time, Kikkoman could see the limitations of a marketing strategy that was aimed only at Asians or Asian Americans living in the United States. For one thing, as Asians living in the United States assimilated into the multifarious stew that was America, their consumption of soy sauce would decline. To ensure continued success, therefore, Kikkoman would have to broaden its market base.

It was a subtle shift, but it was one that Kikkoman sensed almost immediately. Popular films produced in the 1950s such as *Sayonara, Love Is a Many Splendored Thing, The Bridges at Toko-Ri, The World of Suzy Wong, The Barbarian and the Geisha,* and *Escapade in Japan* had helped to create a miniboom for things Asian and Japanese in the United States and Europe. Japanese and Chinese food in particular were finding greater acceptance among non-Japanese and non-Asian Americans. Americans quickly learned that you can't flavor the delicate dishes of Asia with ketchup and barbecue sauce. Only soy sauce could enhance most of the subtle flavors of Japan and China. It was time to drive that point home via an accelerated advertising and marketing campaign.

What better way to do that than during that most American of American events—the presidential election. In 1956, Kikkoman's San Francisco office bought airtime during network coverage of the elections. As Americans watched the returns roll in between Republican incumbent President Dwight D. Eisenhower and Democratic challenger, Adlai Stevenson, they were also treated to the first-ever televised ads for Kikkoman Soy Sauce. The TV ads eventually resulted in an order from Safeway—the first major American supermarket chain to carry Kikkoman Soy Sauce.

Mogi, who in 1961 became the first Japanese to receive an MBA from Columbia University's Graduate School of Business, had lived in the United States long enough to see the potential for Japan's ancient condiment. Americans were open-minded and venturesome when it came to trying new foods and tastes. He found that out when, as a student at Columbia, he demonstrated the use of soy sauce at the 1959 International Trade Fair in Chicago.

"We cooked some meat with soy sauce, cut it into small pieces, and asked people to try it," Mogi recalled. "The response was very positive. People liked the taste. I enjoyed that work. It was good experience for me. I learned that demonstrating a product is a very effective method of sales promotion."

Mogi continued to do demonstrations—often at supermarkets on weekends—until he graduated. But creating and maintaining new markets for soy sauce, while important, are not what will keep Kikkoman on the leading edge in the long run. Indeed, only 50 percent of Kikkoman's revenues are generated by soy sauce. The key to Kikkoman's future lies in the continued globalization and customization of its products as well as expanded research and development in biotechnology and genetic engineering.

The push to globalize and customize its products continued on March 5, 1997, when Kikkoman broke ground for its newest plant in Folsom, California. The Folsom site will be Kikkoman's second soy sauce manufacturing facility in the United States, and it will help the company provide more product for the U.S. and Canadian markets. The $40-million Folsom facility will initially turn out some 2.6 million gal of soy sauce per year when it goes into production in the fall of 1998, but over the next 20 years, its capacity could rise to 20 million gal—just slightly less than Kikkoman's Walworth, Wisconsin, plant.

The groundbreaking was the culmination of a 2-year search by Kikkoman and PHH Fantus Consulting for a site to build a new West Coast facility. In the end, "Project Windward," as Fantus dubbed the exercise, came down to a choice between Folsom and Corvallis, Oregon. Fantus, which specializes in site selections for manufacturers and other businesses, scoured the western United States before picking Corvallis and Folsom as the finalists. More than 150 counties in Washington, Oregon, California, and Nevada were scouted. Eventually, Fantus narrowed the choices to nine sites and then two.

The criteria were the same as those used to select Kikkoman's Walworth facility in 1972: plenty of fresh air, clean water, a reliable work force, and room to grow. In the end, the decision to select Folsom over Corvallis came down to proximity to market. Even though land was more expensive in Folsom than in Corvallis (Kikkoman paid about $5 million for 52 acres in Folsom's Silverbrook Industrial Park area), the fact that Folsom was closer to Kikkoman's major markets in San Francisco and Los Angeles was a key factor, said Milton Neshek, general counsel for Kikkoman Foods, Inc., Kikkoman's U.S. subsidiary.

Of course, Folsom, which is located about 20 mi east of Sacramento, didn't hurt its case by offering an attractive package of incentives. In addition to expediting the permitting process, the city of 40,000 promised a reduction on power rates and a rebate on property taxes generated by the plant and its equipment over an 18-year period. In addition, the state of California offered employment training assistance.

Corvallis, a city of 45,000 about 80 mi south of Portland, was less forthcoming. In fact, it didn't offer any incentives at all, Linda Sarnoff, manager of the city's planning and housing division, told a reporter for the *Sacramento Bee* in 1996.

"We feel we have a high quality of life here," Sarnoff told the reporter. "Those industrial businesses that wish to locate here we welcome, but we will not compromise our standards to bring somebody here."

Neshek and other Kikkoman officials are quick to point out that the economic incentives Folsom offered, while attractive, weren't the critical determining factors.

"Corvallis and Folsom were very comparable in almost all aspects," Neshek said. "Our economic analysis put them pretty equal. In the end, less than $500,000 separated Folsom and Corvallis in terms of cost. We had to make the decision based on noneconomic factors. Folsom really wanted us to be there. They were very aggressive in looking for good clean industry, and soy sauce production fills that bill."

Kikkoman invited Folsom's officials to talk with their counterparts in Walworth, Wisconsin, about the company and its plant there.

"We wanted them to be assured that soy sauce production is a clean, environmentally friendly business," Neshek said.

It was a good move, said Al Gianini, executive director of SACTO, the regional economic recruiter.

"Kikkoman is a flagship name in the food business and Japanese industry," Gianini told a *Sacramento Bee* reporter. "In the food industry worldwide, it has great value...When we say Kikkoman is here, we don't have to explain what that means."

Ultimately, Kikkoman's decision to pick Folsom over Corvallis came down to a matter of geography.

"There was the issue of proximity to our major markets in San Francisco and Los Angeles," said Neshek. "Being closer to those markets means better customer service and shorter delivery times."

But Kikkoman's presence in Folsom is not a one-way deal. According to Fantus, between the plant's construction in 1997 through initial production in 1998, the total cumulative economic impact generated by the Folsom facility will be roughly $152 million. At full production in the next century, total economic impact (excluding Kikkoman's investment but including construction, taxes, payroll, fringe benefits, retail sales, and suppliers) could exceed $325 million. That's not bad for a highly automated plant that will go on line with only about 30 full-time employees. It was also a fact not lost on California Governor Pete Wilson, who wrote three letters to Yuzaburo Mogi encouraging him to locate Kikkoman's new plant in Folsom.

"Japan continues to be California's biggest trading partner," Wilson said. "Our state exported more than $16.5 billion in goods to Japan in 1995. Foreign investments in California by Japanese companies are valued at more than $34 billion and support nearly 200,000 jobs in the state." Wilson noted that Kikkoman opened its first U.S. operation in California in 1957 and that, after 40 years, the company still considers California a good investment.

Even though Kikkoman selected Folsom over Corvallis, the Oregon city didn't walk away empty-handed. Kikkoman paid a development review fee of $3325 to the city. But the city was pleasantly surprised when Neshek hand-delivered a check for $5000 to Corvallis Mayor Helen Berg the day after Kikkoman announced that Folsom was its choice. In a letter to Mayor Berg, Kikkoman asked that the $5000 gift be donated to the Corvallis-Benton County Library for improving technology.

"The people and city officials of Corvallis were great," said Neshek. "We just wanted to show our appreciation."

Mayor Berg, while disappointed that Kikkoman hadn't opted for her city, praised Kikkoman for its thoughtfulness and good corporate citizenship.

"I think it was just good manners," she told the Corvallis *Gazette-Times*. "Corporations are often berated these days. I think it's important to take note of this mannerly action."

While Kikkoman will spend some $40 million to build its new Folsom soy sauce plant, it will spend about $19 million of its $2 billion in annual sales on research and development in areas far removed from the condiments consumers can buy for their tables: pharmaceuticals and biochemicals, including recombinant DNA technology and enzymology. Soy sauce may be the 300-year-old foundation upon which Kikkoman was built, but biotechnology will be a critical pillar for the company's continued growth into the twenty-first century.

2 CHAPTER

From Osaka Castle to the Big Foot Prairie:

A Brief History of Kikkoman

While 1630 is generally accepted as the date when the founding ancestors of today's Kikkoman Corporation settled in Japan's soy sauce producing area, 1615 may have been the most significant year as far as the company's history is concerned. That was the year that the fate of the company's founding matriarch became intricately and tragically intertwined with two of Japan's most powerful warlords and their families: Hideyoshi Toyotomi (1536–1598) and Ieyasu Tokugawa (1543–1616), the founder of Japan's last great feudal house.

On one level, the story of Kikkoman's founding and growth is a story of survival and grit worthy of a sweeping Hollywood epic. But on another, it's a story of quiet endurance, hard work, and consistent effort that spans almost 400 years of Japanese history.

It is impossible to understand the history of a Japanese enterprise as old as Kikkoman without a basic understanding of Japan's last feudal period—an era that lasted from 1603 to 1868, which the Japanese call the "Tokugawa-jidai," or the Tokugawa era. While the Tokugawa era ushered in almost 300 years of relative peace, it did so at the expense of social, technological, and political progress. During the 265 years Japan was governed by the Tokugawa shoguns, the country was literally closed to the rest of the world except for the port of Nagasaki, where Dutch traders were allowed to conduct international commerce.

If we could look through a window at the Japan that existed in 1615, we would see a land far removed from the efficient, high-powered industrial nation of today. The Japan of 1615 was an agrarian-based land held hostage by feudalism. It was a land ruled by constantly feuding warlords, or Daimyo, many of whom only grudgingly declared their allegiance to the Tokugawa Shogunate. Indeed, so tenuous was the shogun's hold on the nation's warlords that they were required to leave their families in Edo (today's Tokyo) as hostages when they weren't there themselves.

It was in this rather precarious climate that we find Shige Maki living in the shadow of Osaka Castle where her husband, Yorinori, was a samurai retainer of Hideyori Toyotomi. Hideyori (1593–1615) was the son of Hideyoshi Toyotomi, one of Japan's greatest warlords and a man credited with uniting Japan in 1590 by subjugating the five western provinces of Japan's main island of Honshu. In recognition of this incredible feat, Toyotomi was given the title lieutenant general by Japan's emperor—a position which effectively gave him absolute power over the Japanese archipelago.

In 1586, Hideyoshi had built magnificent Osaka Castle—the largest and most impressive castle in Japan. At its peak, the castle and its outer defenses measured 2 mi from east to west and 1.5 mi from north to south. It took more than 60,000 laborers 2 years to build the complex, which has been reconstructed and which attracts thousands of visitors each day.

For the next 5 years, Hideyoshi Toyotomi continued to consolidate his power via a series of battles and castle sieges. In 1591, he issued an edict establishing four distinct classes of people. At the top were samurai, followed by farmers, artisans, and merchants. That social pecking order would freeze social mobility throughout Japan until 1868 when Japan's emperor Meiji ended feudalism and ushered in the nation's modern era.

Not satisfied with ruling Japan, in 1597 Hideyoshi led a force of 150,000 onto the Korean peninsula. His objective: to conquer Korea and China. His experienced army defeated combined Korean and Chinese forces, but in 1598, with victory in sight, Hideyoshi became ill and died. Japanese forces were withdrawn from Korea, and in 1600, Ieyasu Tokugawa, a senior general in Hideyoshi's army seized power following the battle of Sekigahara when he defeated an army of former Hideyoshi vassals and retainers.

It was a move that was viewed as treachery by many of Hideyoshi's former supporters. As with other generals, Ieyasu Tokugawa had given his word to Hideyoshi as he lay dying in 1598 that he would support and protect his son Hideyori—just 6 years old at the time. In 1603, Ieyasu Tokugawa was awarded the title of shogun by the emperor—a title which translates as "great barbarian-subduing general." The closest Western equivalent is the Spanish word "generalissimo."

Even though Ieyasu Tokugawa was now the undisputed military ruler of Japan, the split between him and the Toyotomi family grew wider. In 1611, Tokugawa was convinced that the Toyotomi family, now led by 19-year-old Hideyori, represented a serious challenge to the legitimacy of his rule. Not even a marriage arranged that year between Ieyasu's granddaughter Sen Hime and Hideyori resolved the lingering hostility.

Like most Japanese in this feudal world, Shige Maki and her husband, Yorinori, were little more than pawns in a complex, kabukilike struggle for power. They and other Hideyori supporters knew that it was only a matter of time until the houses of Tokugawa and Toyotomi met in violent conflict.

Sure enough, in 1614, 3 years after Tokugawa sent his granddaughter into Osaka Castle, the old shogun accused Hideyori of subversive behavior. Hideyori responded by assembling an army of 100,000 around his castle. Many of them were *ronin,* or unemployed samurai, who saw the coming battle as an opportunity to improve their fortunes. In January 1615, Ieyasu Tokugawa and his son, Hidetada, led an army of 200,000 men against the Toyotomi stronghold.

Several probing attacks against the castle soon confirmed just how impregnable the fortress was. Built on a high hill overlooking the river Yodogawa, the castle was constructed on a base of massive granite stones that sloped steeply upward to the main compound. After weeks of fighting, Ieyasu withdrew, but before he did, he filled in the outer moats of the castle, thus rendering the castle's defenses less formidable.

In the spring, Ieyasu issued an ultimatum to Hideyori: He could either discharge his army of samurai warriors or he could move to another province. Hideyori refused to follow either course, and in the spring of 1615, Ieyasu sent another army of 200,000 men to Osaka. This time, with the castle's defenses less effective, Hideyori's army was forced to meet Ieyasu's forces on the open battlefield, where they were routed.

The beginning of the end for Hideyori came on June 3, 1615. With Hideyori's main force defeated, Ieyasu's army had little trouble overwhelming Osaka Castle. The next day, in a castle tower that had held out, Hideyori and his mother committed suicide. Hideyori's 7-year-old son, Kunimatsu (by a concubine, not by Tokugawa's granddaughter), was beheaded—lest he grow up to become an enemy of the Tokugawa Shogunate.

This was the world that Shige Maki found herself living in. It was a world further complicated by her own husband's death following the siege of Osaka Castle. Along with several other Toyotomi retainers and warriors who were distraught at having failed their lord, Yorinori committed suicide.

One can only imagine the scene around Osaka Castle during those hot summer days of June 1615. While portions of the castle still smoldered, high-ranking supporters of Toyotomi were being rounded up and beheaded—often along with their wives and children. Recorded accounts reveal that the carnage was extremely horrific.

Even though her husband had already committed suicide, Shige Maki knew that if she and her young son, Heizaburo, were caught, they would probably be put to the sword. She had to escape. Possibly disguising themselves as peasants, Shige Maki and her son slipped out of the castle amid the bloodshed and confusion. For 15 years, the pair was on the run while loyal retainers of the Tokugawa Shogunate scoured the land for former Toyotomi followers. Eventually, Shige Maki and Heizaburo settled in the small farming community of Noda, about 30 mi north of Edo (now Tokyo). In the interim, they had changed their name from Maki to Mogi, with Heizaburo altering his first name to Shichizaemon.

No descriptions of Shige Maki exist, but she must have been one tough and resourceful lady. Not only did she survive the bloody battle of Osaka Castle and outwit the shogun's henchmen, but she spent years working in the rice fields of Noda. Rice cultivation in feudal Japan was backbreaking, labor-intensive work. Threshing, hulling, weeding, and the transplanting of seedlings were mostly accomplished with human labor, often to the tune of 600 worker-hours per acre, according to the *Kodansha Encyclopedia of Japan.* Even today, rice cultivation remains a heavily labor-intensive pursuit, with an average of more than 300 worker-hours of labor required for each acre under cultivation in Japan—about 40 times more than are required for corn cultivation in the United States.

The Tokugawa Shogunate's theory of economics was straightforward and brutal in the seventeenth and eighteenth centuries. Because agriculture was the primary source of wealth in Japan's agrarian-based economy, it was tightly controlled. It was a harsh economic system that allowed farmers to keep just enough of what they produced to live on and to use as seed for next year's crop. Everything else was taken from them as tax. Farmers were even forbidden to drink tea or sake or to burn leaves for fuel. Everything was to be turned over to the authorities. Peasant revolts, often led by ronin, erupted often and were just as often brutally crushed.

It is little wonder, then, that some farmers became intrigued with the art of *shoyu,* or soy sauce, fermentation. For one thing, producing shoyu had to be easier than stooping all day in rice paddies only to see the fruits of one's labor carted off by the shogun's minions. Shoyu as we know it today first appeared in Japan in the mid-1500s. Before that, a thick, black forerunner known as *miso-tamari* had been the condiment of choice in Japan. Miso-tamari had its origins in another soybean-based condiment imported from China called *chiang,* or *hishio,* in Japanese. These condiments are more akin to the *nuoc mam* fish sauce still used today in Vietnam and the *naam pla* sauce found in Thailand.

Soybean-based foods such as *tofu* (soybean curd) and *miso* (fermented soybean paste) made their appearance in Japan in the midseventh century. Miso-tamari was apparently introduced to Japan in the midthirteenth century by a Japanese Zen priest named Kakushin who had learned how to make miso while studying in China. After the priest returned to the Kokoku-ji temple near Yuasa, just south of Osaka, and began making miso, he discovered that by heating miso to stop fermentation and by adding more water, he could create a liquid seasoning. Because it was skimmed off the top of miso vats during fermentation, it came to be known as miso-tamari. Shoyu evolved following years of experimenting with methods of fermentation and with the primary ingredients of miso-tamari.

Shoyu was much different from the heavier, thicker, and sweeter miso-tamari. Whereas miso-tamari was made from a mash of cooked soybeans, salt, and water, shoyu was fermented from soybeans, salt, water, and a new ingredient: roasted and cracked wheat. As a result, the new shoyu had a deeper, darker color and a much more delicate flavor and aroma. Japanese historians generally concede that this new method of making shoyu was first devised in Choshi, a small fishing village about 50 mi east of what is now Tokyo, according to research by the Soyfoods Center of California.

There was just one problem, however. Shoyu was much more expensive than the miso-tamari condiment that Japan's population had been using since the fourteenth century. Shoyu required more sophisticated equipment. For example, it had to be pressed in a vat with a pressing machine and run off through a spigot. For much of the seventeenth century, shoyu was considered a luxury and its use was limited mostly to the country's wealthy nobility.

In fact, shoyu's popularity didn't begin to spread until after more and more Japanese began moving from rural areas into the cities. Before the onset of the Tokugawa Shogunate in 1603, only about 2 percent of Japan's population lived in cities. By the early eighteenth century, that figure had climbed to 20 percent. This dramatic shift in Japan's demographics also increased the demand for shoyu in its rapidly growing urban centers such as Edo, Osaka, and Kyoto. Nevertheless, shoyu production during the mid-seventeenth century was still largely a cottage industry confined to the winter months when rice could not be cultivated.

But as demand for the new condiment grew, more and more small family-operated shoyu businesses began to spring up. Among the earliest recorded shoyu producers in the Noda area were Hyozaemon Takanashi and Shichizaemon Mogi. Local records show that Takanashi was producing fermented shoyu in 1661, while the Mogis were making miso.

A year later, on August 22, 1662, some 47 years after she had escaped from the ruins of Osaka Castle, Shige Maki died. There is no doubt that if Shige Maki had not been as intrepid and resourceful as she was, there would be no Kikkoman Corporation today. In all likelihood, she and her son would have perished during the siege of Osaka Castle and the Mogi clan would have ended right there before it had the opportunity to produce even one bottle of soy sauce.

During the next several decades, the business relationship between the Takanashi and Mogi families grew closer, culminating in the marriage in 1768 of the eldest son of the Hyozaemon Takanashi clan with the daughter of the fifth generation Shichizaemon Mogi line. This was to be only the first in a series of alliances between the Mogi and Takanashi families that were designed to perpetuate both families. As is frequently the case in Japan, the son-in-law was "adopted" by the Mogi family and assumed the Mogi name. This system of *muko-yoshi,* or "son-in-law adoption," is not some antiquated procedure, but continues today in modern Japan when there is no male heir to continue the family name.

In this first case of son-in-law adoption and consanguineous marriages between the Mogi and Takanashi families, the newlyweds established a shoyu factory, and by 1768, the alliance was recognized as the Kashiwa branch of the Mogi family. Between 1764 and 1822, no less than five separate Mogi households had entered into shoyu production in Noda. A sixth branch began in 1872 and a seventh in 1900. While the branches of the Mogi family grew, by the end of the nineteenth century only one branch of the Takanashi family was still involved in shoyu production.

It's only through this system of muko-yoshi that the Mogi name has managed to survive the many generations that have followed the family's beginnings in seventeenth-century Noda. While the Mogi name has been perpetuated, the muko-yoshi system has also created a complex family genealogy that has resulted in a main Mogi household and several Mogi branches. For example, the system of muko-yoshi means there is no direct bloodline to Shige Maki, the original Mogi matriarch, as there is among the royal households of Europe or Japan. Yuzaburo Mogi, Kikkoman's president and CEO, is a good example of how this system works in actual practice.

"My grandfather Keizaburo had no children, so he adopted my mother, who was the daughter of his nephew," Mogi explained. "In 1929, my mother married my father, who was then adopted into the Mogi family and changed his name to Keizaburo Mogi—the same as my grandfather."

Mogi's father was born Katsuji Iida in 1899 in the town of Asahi in Chiba Prefecture. The son of a farmer, Katsuji's ambitions extended far beyond the family farm. Before he met Mogi's mother, he had gone to Tokyo Shoka University, the predecessor of today's Hitotsubashi University, to study business. After graduation, he was offered a job with Mitsui & Co. and would have joined Mitsui if one of his professors hadn't convinced him to join Kikkoman instead.

Kikkoman, which at the time was called the Noda Shoyu Co., was embroiled in a major labor dispute. Keizaburo had specialized in labor relations at the university and the professor insisted that he would be a better fit at the company that eventually would become Kikkoman than at Mitsui. He wasn't wrong. In April 1926, Keizaburo joined Kikkoman, and a year later, his university training was put to the test. Beginning in April 1927 and continuing for 218 days, some 3500 Noda Shoyu employees went on strike demanding 10 percent wage increases for men and 20 percent for women. In all, a list of six demands was presented to the company's leadership. It was the longest strike in prewar Japanese history. Eventually, 1100 workers would be fired, though 30 percent of them were eventually rehired. Among the positives to come out of the strike was the suggestion by Keizaburo Mogi that Kikkoman adopt a *sangyo-damashii,* or corporate philosophy, that embodied the spirit of the company.

"The sangyo-damashii held that an enterprise is a public institution," explained Keizaburo Mogi, who served as president of the company from 1962 to 1974 when he became chairman of the board. "We have a very important obligation to serve consumers and society through our business. It is our mission and the great principle of management, which eventually will bring happiness."

For Kikkoman's sangyo-damashii to be more than a few hollow words tacked on the wall of the company's factories and offices, the company would have to stress efficiency, profitability, and high wages, said Keizaburo Mogi, who died in 1993. In essence, the new corporate philosophy created a new social contract with labor—a social contract that restructured work practices and introduced new management systems that were geared to reward employees for their performance in addition to their tenure. At the same time, it reorganized production processes to accommodate new technologies. The object, Keizaburo Mogi explained at the time, was to convince employees that their best interests and those of Kikkoman were one in the same.

In effect, Kikkoman was inviting its employees to become part of the 300-year-old Mogi family. This *ikka,* or one-family philosophy, is still very strong within Kikkoman—a remarkable achievement given the company's rapid pace of internationalization. Workers in the company's Walworth, Wisconsin, plant feel as much a part of the Kikkoman family as those turning out the Kikkoman shoyu that is brewed specially for Japan's imperial family.

Ken Hill, a foreman who has worked since 1974 at Kikkoman's Walworth, Wisconsin, plant, put it as well as anybody: "Kikkoman considers all of us to be part of its family. Even my wife and son are considered part of the Kikkoman family. You are treated with a great deal of respect here and you know the company sincerely appreciates what you are doing."

Hill's sentiments are echoed by workers in Noda, many of whom are descendants of the men and women who took part in what is known in Japanese history as the Great Noda Strike of 1927–1928.

"I'm very satisfied here," said Koichi Endo, who has worked almost 40 years for Kikkoman and is currently assistant manager of the pressing division of the Noda soy sauce plant. "I feel responsible for making good quality soy sauce, and to me that's very satisfying."

Not far from Endo, a bottling line sent 500 plastic 1-L bottles of soy sauce per minute hurtling toward a machine which packed them 12 to a box. The plant turns out 1 million 1-L bottles each day.

"This is a good place to work," Endo continued. "It's like being part of a very old and respected family."

Yaeko Hayase and Kazuko Kozuka, both of whom work in the product development department of Kikkoman's research and development center in Noda and who were instrumental in developing Kikkoman's newest product (a new soy sauce-based meat sauce called

Yakiniku-no-Tare), say they feel like "Kikkoman mothers" when they are working on a new product.

"It's like being part of a big family...and everybody feels part of it," said Kazuko.

While it would be inaccurate to say that today's far-flung Kikkoman Corporation is the same as those small family businesses that sprang up during the early years of the Tokugawa Shogunate, the company has nevertheless worked hard to maintain a sense of family even as it has expanded into nearly 100 countries.

The evolution of today's Kikkoman Corporation can be broken down into four separate periods. The first era, as already described, begins in 1630 with Shige Maki settling in Noda and continues until the late nineteenth century. During this initial phase, the production of shoyu by the Mogi clans was primarily accomplished via small family enterprises that sprang up around Noda. These small enterprises grew not only because of the quality of the shoyu but because of Noda's auspicious geographic location. Not only were soybeans and wheat grown in the area, but Noda was only a 1-day trip on the Edo River from Tokyo. By the mideighteenth century, Tokyo was probably the largest city in the world. It had more than 1 million inhabitants and sprawled in a broad crescent around Tokyo Bay. That meant easily accessible, reliable, and most important, growing markets for the shoyu the Mogis and others were making in Noda.

One Mogi branch, headed by Saheiji Mogi, made a particularly shrewd move in 1838. Saheiji applied for and received official trademark recognition of his family's premier brand name from the shogun. The name? Kikkoman. Long before there were marketing consultants to tell him such things, Saheiji Mogi began promoting brand name recognition and brand loyalty among consumers via an ambitious advertising campaign geared to make the distinctive hexagonal Kikkoman logo recognized everywhere. Mogi sponsored professional sumo wrestlers and distributed paper lanterns and umbrellas embossed with the Kikkoman logo. He even had ornate gold labels made in

Paris so that kegs of Kikkoman shoyu would stand out from those of his competitors and imitators.

At a time when a closed Japan was just beginning to open its doors to the outside world, Saheiji Mogi was already pushing to internationalize one of Japan's most traditional products. Kegs of Kikkoman shoyu were shipped to Japanese immigrants in Hawaii and California in 1868—the same year that the Emperor Meiji wrested power from the Tokugawa Shogunate and began moving Japan from feudalism to a constitutional government. Thus, long before the world had ever heard of Toyota or Sony or Matsushita, it knew about Kikkoman. In fact, the Kikkoman brand may have been the first Japanese product to achieve international recognition.

In 1872, Mogi entered his soy sauce in the Amsterdam World's Fair, and the next year, he entered it in the Austrian World's Fair where it won a letter of commendation for excellence. In 1879, the Kikkoman brand name was registered in California and in Germany in 1886. By 1906, it was registered in every American state.

By the early and midnineteenth century, the shoyu made by the Mogi and Takanashi families had earned a reputation as among the best in Japan. So prized was the shoyu produced by Noda's brewers, including the Mogi and Takanashi families, that the Japanese government actually exempted many of them from the price controls that regulated other products between 1860 and 1870. The reason? The government decided the Noda shoyu brewers could not maintain the quality of their products if they were forced to reduce prices. Much to Mogi's delight, the government's exemption was perceived as the shogun's "stamp of approval" by the public, further enhancing the stature of the Kikkoman brand name.

The second phase in Kikkoman's development was a critical 30-year span between 1887 and 1917—an era marked by Japan's rapid industrialization. But almost as important, as far as the seven branches of the Mogi family were concerned, was the problem of intensified competition. By 1910, for example, Japanese records show that no fewer than 9000 companies were making soy sauce in Japan. It didn't take long for the shoyu market to become saturated with product. Market prices plummeted and even the Mogi family's prized Kikkoman label could no longer command prices that were often two and three times those of competitors. Raw materials and labor costs fluctuated wildly as thousands of small brewers battled one another for market share.

It was obvious that things couldn't continue. And they didn't. In 1887, brewers from Noda took action. Twelve of them formed the Noda Shoyu Brewers' Association. The association agreed to work together to: (1) purchase raw materials such as soybeans, wheat, and salt in volume; (2) standardize wages in the industry; and (3) regulate the amount of shoyu they sent to market. The collective power of the association allowed its members to outproduce and outmarket other shoyu competitors who sold product in the Tokyo area. Eventually, association members captured about 10 percent of the Tokyo market—the largest single share of any shoyu market in Japan.

The association was also able to take advantage of another development in Japan: the advent of a national railway system. During this 30-year period of Kikkoman's development, the Japanese government had managed to create a national rail system that linked most of the nation's major metropolitan areas. By joining forces and sharing the cost, the Noda Shoyu Brewers' Association was able to defray the cost of building a local railway spur from Noda to the national rail system. Once that was accomplished, the association began importing raw materials needed for shoyu production. Through a system of bulk buying and shipping, it was not only able to control costs, but also to ensure a better quality of salt, soybeans, and wheat, which were imported from countries such as Korea, China, England, and Canada.

In 1904, it also set up and funded a joint research and development laboratory to study and improve shoyu production. It analyzed new fermentation technology, examined ways to improve quality, and introduced new processes that leveraged new mechanization methods.

Kikkoman corporate lore says that in 1907 one member of the Mogi family (Shinzaburo Mogi) moved to the United States and started a shoyu factory in Denver, Colorado, perhaps hoping to find new untapped markets in America. The factory apparently failed, and Mogi, who was born in 1872, moved to Chicago where he became involved in the trading business.

By 1909, one branch of the Mogi family (Yuuemon Mogi) had put up Japan's first fully mechanized shoyu factory and had dramatically reduced the time needed to ferment shoyu from about 22 months to 16. Soon, members of the association were exporting shoyu to Korea and China as well as to Japanese immigrants in Hawaii and California.

Something else happened during this period. Consumers began to demand shoyu in smaller glass containers rather than in traditional wooden barrels that were difficult to store and tended to leak.

As effective as the association was, it soon became apparent to members of the various shoyu-producing Mogi families that by joining forces they could become even more productive and profitable. In 1917, six Mogi families and one Takanashi family withdrew from the association and formed the Noda Shoyu Company. The Horikiri family joined 1 month later.

One of the first orders of business for the new company, in addition to setting up the company's management structure and its sales, distribution, and production departments, was to decide on a name for its soy sauce. After months of debate, discussion, and haggling, the new company decided that Kikkoman—the shoyu that Saheiji Mogi had made famous through his aggressive advertising and promotion campaigns in the nineteenth century—would be the flagship product of the new company. Even though the eight families that formed the new company hoped that one of their brands would be the flagship of the new company, they realized that in order to succeed, Noda Shoyu needed to standardize its products. At the time of the merger, the eight Mogi and Takanashi families were making 200 different brands of shoyu—including Kikkoman. While it continued to make a few other brands to satisfy certain regional tastes in the Japanese market, Kikkoman was the brand that received most of the money and talent.

During the next 10 years, Noda Shoyu launched an aggressive modernization program designed to introduce new manufacturing and fermentation processes. Hydraulic presses, conveyors, elevators, boilers, and steel vats were brought in. Human labor was replaced with machines. Advances in biotechnology resulted in the accelerated fermentation of shoyu.

While these advances dramatically improved productivity at the company's plants, they also sowed the seeds of the 218-day labor dispute that would erupt in 1927, which would ultimately set the company on a course of social responsibility that it still follows today.

In Noda, entire families were employed by the Noda Shoyu Co., and its leaders, the Mogis and Takanashis, were regarded as patriarchs of a vast corporate family. It was a responsibility that company leaders took seriously. Noda Shoyu provided financial support for dozens of civic enterprises, including the town's cultural center, its library, fire station, hospital, schools, and various recreational facilities. It even built a large portion of the town's water system. In return, the company built up an incredible amount of goodwill and social capital, not to mention a loyal and reliable work force.

The Noda Shoyu Co. was in effect a mini-zaibatsu—a grouping of interrelated enterprises. It controlled a half-dozen shoyu enterprises and four others that were involved in the financial and transportation industries. It would remain that way until the end of World War II in 1945, when U.S. occupation forces abolished the laws of the Meiji Constitution that permitted the existence of zaibatsu. Under the old Meiji code, the concept of *kokutai,* or patriarchal state with the emperor as father, became the guiding philosophy of the country. It permeated every aspect of Japanese life—from business to sports to education.

The era between 1917 and 1941 brought tremendous economic expansion to the new company. International markets were exploited to take advantage of the company's increased production of Kikkoman brand shoyu. Sales offices were set up throughout Asia, and import-export agents helped the Noda Shoyu Co. sell Kikkoman Soy Sauce in Europe, the United States, and South America.

Eventually, it set up factories in Inchon, Korea, and Beijing, China, and by 1939, the company was exporting 10 percent of its annual production with 5 percent going to Asian markets and another 5 percent to Hawaii and California. Japanese government records show that 99 percent of Japan's shoyu exports in 1939 carried the Kikkoman label, according to *Kikkoman, Company, Clan, and Community,* a 1983 case study of the company by California State University Hayward History professor, W. Mark Fruin.

While the first three centuries of Kikkoman's existence saw a small family-owned enterprise survive the challenges of feudalism and the Industrial Revolution to evolve into a major Japanese company, the five decades since the end of World War II have been just as challenging.

During the U.S. military occupation, Japan's entire business system was turned on its ear. Zaibatsu were forbidden, as were the collaborative marketing and distribution agreements created in prewar days between Japan's four major shoyu manufacturers: Noda Shoyu Co., Higeta, Yamasa, and Marukin. Shoyu exports were also banned until 1949. But most serious of all was something that had never happened before in Japan: Per capita demand for shoyu was declining. Why? For one thing, postwar Japanese families were smaller. But there was something else at work in Japan. In addition to their chewing gum, chocolate, and nylons, American GIs were introducing new kinds of food to the Japanese. Until the end of World War II, most Japanese ate fish, rice, and vegetables more than anything else. In the years following World War II, diets began to change. Suddenly, Japanese were eating red meat, bread, and dairy products—foods that didn't require shoyu.

During the war, the quality of Kikkoman Soy Sauce suffered because the company was unable to obtain the soybeans, wheat, and other ingredients necessary to manufacture fermented shoyu. But although the war was devastating to the company (as it was to just about every Japanese enterprise), Noda Shoyu demonstrated remarkable resilience and innovation. Among other things, its researchers and scientists discovered that in lieu of soybeans they could use copra to make soy sauce. It was a process the company shared with other shoyu brewers during the war.

The company also began to make seminaturally brewed soy sauce. Whereas fermented or brewed soy sauce takes months to make, chemically produced shoyu can be produced in just hours by boiling soybeans in hydrochloric acid, filtering it, and adding corn syrup, salt, and caramel coloring. While the taste and aroma are nowhere near those of naturally fermented soy sauce, it is nevertheless much less expensive to manufacture and requires fewer essential ingredients.

With Japanese eating habits shifting, the Noda Shoyu Co. wasted no time in returning to its traditional shoyu brewing methods after the war. As soon as it could import the raw materials it needed, it was once again turning out high-quality Kikkoman shoyu. But it did something else, too—something that would have a significant impact on Japan's soy sauce brewers and would propel the Noda Shoyu Co. to a position of leadership in the industry that it has never relinquished.

When World War II ended, there were no fewer than 5000 competing soy sauce brewers in Japan, but Kikkoman was far and away the most aggressive in developing and promoting new soy sauce manufacturing technology. Indeed, it would have been possible for the company to have used its new technologies to steamroll many of its competitors—crushing them and buying them out for a fraction of their worth. For example, Kikkoman had developed several new technologies designed to improve and speed up the critical soy sauce fermentation process. These developments alone would have afforded Kikkoman a competitive advantage that would have devastated many smaller regional soy sauce brewers.

But instead of using its new technology as a blunt instrument to bludgeon its competitors into submission, it chose a different route. Rather than seek exclusive patent protection for its new technologies, Kikkoman decided to share them with its competitors. In today's supercompetitive business environment, a decision like that seems rather quaint and even foolhardy. But Kikkoman chose to share its technology with other manufacturers for several reasons—not the least of which were the economic policies of the U.S. occupation forces, headed by General Douglas MacArthur. General headquarters (GHQ) wanted to revive Japan's soy sauce manufacturing industry, which during the war had resorted to using substitute materials.

While Kikkoman didn't feel it could let down many companies that it had formed relationships with that went back centuries, it also didn't want to see Japan's soy sauce industry change from one that relied primarily on natural brewing technology to one that resorted to chemical production.

But there was another reason—one that reflects an ongoing commitment to public service and social responsibility. Specifically, the company's leaders felt that it was their duty to make sure that a reliable supply of top-quality fermented soy sauce was available to the Japanese public, which was still recovering from the devastation of World War II.

Even with its immense production capacity, Kikkoman knew it couldn't supply all of Japan, so the only way to ensure that the public would have enough soy sauce was to increase the productivity of its competitors. Skeptics might challenge Kikkoman's benevolence and wonder if there were any self-serving motives lurking in the wings. Actually, there was a quid pro quo. Kikkoman reasoned that if there was not enough high-quality soy sauce to go around in the years immediately following the war, consumers might lose their taste for soy sauce, and that, in turn, would adversely impact the company's future.

It proved to be a shrewd bit of thinking on Kikkoman's part. Not only did it raise the company's esteem in the eyes of the public and government, but the decision to share its technology did indeed result in increased soy sauce production and consumption at a time when many Japanese were embracing new Western foods brought to Japan by American GIs.

But Kikkoman knew that simply producing high-quality shoyu wouldn't be enough to increase brand recognition in, Japan. It would have to do something else. In the early 1950s, it created a new planning and marketing department to coordinate a three-pronged strategy that included marketing research, advertising, and consumer education. This was critical, because unlike today, in the early 1950s, some 85 percent of the company's profits were derived from soy sauce.

Among other things, the company determined that it would have to market shoyu not only as a traditional Japanese condiment, but as a seasoning for the Western foods that were growing increasingly popular in Japan. It sponsored cooking programs on television that demonstrated shoyu's effectiveness as a seasoning on red meat and other non-Japanese foods. It sent "shoyu squads" door to door to personally demonstrate to Japanese housewives how soy sauce could be used on a variety of foods. It provided soy sauce to Japanese brides-to-be who enrolled in prenuptial cooking classes. The strategy worked. From a 14 percent market share in 1952, Kikkoman's market penetration in the Japanese market has grown to 30 percent today, despite the fact that there are still 2000 soy sauce manufacturers in Japan.

At the same time, since the 1950s and 1960s, the company has diversified its products far beyond soy sauce. Today, barely 50 percent of the company's $2 billion in revenues are generated by the sale of shoyu. In 1949, the company produced seven branded products, according to the 1983 case study by Fruin. Today, it sells some 2500. It also makes 20 different types of shoyu, including one that is specifically brewed at a special facility in Noda for Japan's imperial family.

In 1963, along with Mitsui & Co. and Del Monte Corp., Kikkoman established a joint venture to sell Del Monte products in Japan. In 1990, Kikkoman acquired the Far Eastern division of Del Monte (less the Philippines) from Philip Morris Corp.

The company has also invested in a broad array of businesses, from pharmaceuticals and food-processing machinery to restaurants and genetic engineering. There probably has been more substantive change in the company since 1945 than in its previous 300 years.

One of the most significant changes was the decision in 1964 to change the name of the company from Noda Shoyu Co. to the Kikkoman Shoyu Co. It was a move designed to reflect the company's broader focus and to further capitalize on the Kikkoman brand name, which by now was widely recognized in the United States.

Another significant decision was made in 1970. That was the year Kikkoman determined that sales of its soy sauce in the United States were sufficient to warrant the construction of a U.S. manufacturing facility. Yuzaburo Mogi, who at the time was chief planner for corporate planning, had been studying the possibility since 1965.

"The main reason for building a plant in the United States was that we buy and import our raw materials—soybeans and wheat—from U.S. suppliers," Mogi recalled. "With U.S. sales increasing, it made more sense to make the soy sauce there rather than import the raw materials to Japan and then export the finished product back to America. By making soy sauce in the United States, we would save ocean freight costs and reduce inventory."

While that seems logical enough, it was nevertheless a tough sell among Kikkoman's more conservative board members.

"I had confidence that the U.S. factory would become profitable, but many people didn't believe me," Mogi said.

Eventually, following several board meetings, Mogi's father, Keizaburo, who was Kikkoman's president, gave the go-ahead. From more than 60 midwestern sites—most of them in Wisconsin and Illinois—one 200-acre parcel of land on the outskirts of the small town of Walworth, Wisconsin, was selected.

Ground was broken in January 1972, and in June 1973, the plant was up and running. Today, the 500,000-ft^2 facility is one of Kikkoman's most productive plants anywhere, turning out some 18 million gal of soy sauce and 17 other Kikkoman condiments and products annually.

Walworth, which sits smack in the middle of Wisconsin's Big Foot Prairie on what was once the turf of the Potowatomi Indians, is not only thousands of miles from Japan. In many ways, it is light-years away from the culture and country that first created shoyu. But despite the plant's physical and cultural distance from Japan, you can't help feeling that Shige Maki would appreciate and applaud the risk her descendants took more than 350 years after she fled the flames of Osaka Castle.

3

CHAPTER

A Global Company With a Japanese Soul

During the past three decades, consumers worldwide have gotten used to seeing a wide range of Japanese-made products just about everywhere. Japanese TV sets, VCRs, CD players, and other electronic gear occupy store shelves from Bangkok to Baltimore. By the same token, Japanese cars, trucks, and vans ply the roads on every continent of the world. In the United States alone, there are seven Japanese automobile plants turning out more than 1 million cars each year. This is not news. Japanese companies such as Sony, Matsushita, Mitsubishi, Honda, Toyota, and Sanyo have earned a reputation as first-class, international manufacturers.

But what many people may not have stopped to contemplate as they plug in that big-screen Sony TV or slide behind the wheel of that Lexus 300 is a rather often overlooked fact about the products these companies turn out. Most Japanese companies that have been successful in foreign markets have sold products that originated in the West—automobiles, consumer electronics, machine tools, and so on. Kikkoman is one of a handful of Japanese companies that has been able to take a uniquely Japanese product and sell it in the international marketplace.

This observation was first made in 1979 by Yousuke Kinugasa in a Japanese-language book titled *Internationalization Strategy of Japanese Companies.* Kinugasa, who is director of the Institute of International Business at Japan's Kanagawa University, compared the strategies of three Japanese companies in his book: Honda, Matsushita, and Kikkoman.

"Honda and Matsushita didn't push exports to America with a unique product, but provided known, basically Western products that fit into the U.S. market," Kinugasa said. "On the other hand, Kikkoman was able to take a uniquely Japanese product and then go international with it by creating new markets. Naturally brewed Japanese soy sauce was a new product in the U.S. market when Kikkoman began exporting it there in earnest after World War II."

Professor Kinugasa is not alone in that observation. Hiroo Takahashi, director of research at the Business Research Institute, a Tokyo think tank, has also watched Kikkoman closely and considers it a model for internationalizing a uniquely Japanese product.

"The products that Kikkoman markets internationally originated in Japan, while most other Japanese companies sell products that originated in the West," Takahashi observed. "Those Western-originated products are really based on technology developed in Europe and America. But shoyu is based on technology that evolved in Japan for hundreds of years. And it's a product with a uniquely Japanese taste."

How Kikkoman managed to create a market for a little-known Japanese product like shoyu in the United States and nearly 100 other countries is considered one of the wonders of the Japanese business world. How it was able to actually expand and grow those markets is even more astounding to those who follow the activities of Japanese companies.

Some say Kikkoman's success in the international marketplace is a result of good planning and research.

Others say it was astute marketing and dogged persistence. Still others insist it was due to a rare mix of aggressive leadership in a traditionally conservative company that resulted in an ability to take well-calculated risks. In fact, it is probably all of the above—and something else, too.

More than 70 years ago, the six Mogi families and the Takanashi and Horikiri families adopted a written family code of business. It's an informal 17-point document that has played an important role in Kikkoman's corporate governance since eight families merged to create the company in 1917.

The Mogi family creed is much more ambitious than one of those pithy vision statements that so many companies create only to hang on their office walls these days. While portions of it may seem quaint and outdated, each article contains a nugget of underlying truth. For that reason, it remains a document that members of the Mogi family still conduct their professional and private lives by. It reads:

1. *Family members should recognize that harmony is of utmost importance. Harmony fosters mutual respect which permits family members to focus on prosperity in business and on the longevity of the fortunes of the families.*

2. *Worshipping and respecting a Supreme Being is the foundation for nurturing virtue. Keeping faith nourishes your own mind.*

3. *Loyalty and patriotism are an obligation. Respect and serve your country and observe the fundamental character of your country.*

4. *Family members should recognize that courtesy is a fundamental element. If, as a senior member, you lack courtesy, junior family members will not give allegiance to you. If junior members lack courtesy, there may be serious repercussions. Mutual courtesy will result in a self-governing, peaceful family.*

5. *Always keep in mind that virtue is the origin and wealth is its product. Do not judge a person by his wealth or lack of wealth.*

6. *Strict discipline should be maintained. Evaluate each employee with fairness. Demand the utmost in diligence. The hierarchy in any organization must be maintained.*

7. *Human resources are the most valuable treasure of the company. Each employee should be treated without personal prejudice* *and be placed in the most appropriate position according to his capability and achievements. Each employee should be respected and his self-worth should be maintained and enhanced.*

8. *The education of our children is our responsibility to our nation and to our community. The body and the mind should be trained with moral, intellectual, and physical education.*

9. *Benevolence should be extended to all living things. Benevolence is the source for discipline and the mother of virtue. Words are the door to both fortune and misfortune. A harsh tongue can hurt others and also yourself. A kind demeanor will make you feel at ease even in times of turmoil. Be careful of each word you speak.*

10. *Simplicity and frugality have been the time-honored tradition of the family for generations. Live within your means.*

11. *True profit comes from hard work and maximum effort. Speculation is not the best road to follow. Business which is done contrary to social order and by taking advantage of others' weakness should be prohibited.*

12. *Competition is essential to progress. Excessive and unethical competition should be avoided.*

13. *Any judgment should be made clearly and fairly. Rewards and penalties should be fully recognized. Rewards will encourage challenges and penalties will discourage thoughtless mistakes.*

14. *When beginning a new business consult with family members. Do not make decisions by yourself. You should recognize that absence of a business loss is akin to making a profit.*

15. *Do not fall into debt carelessly. Do not act as a guarantor for any loan. Never lend money to make a profit.*

16. *Give as much money from your personal earnings to society as possible. Never ask for a reward or think highly of yourself.*

17. *Do not decide important matters by yourself. Always consult with the people who have a direct interest in the subject matter prior to making a decision. Shared decision-making results in people having a positive attitude in their work.*

While many American corporations all too often tend to dismiss such documents as "soft" tools of management, in Japan they are not taken lightly. Indeed, the Mogi family creed is much more than a collection of obsolete ramblings from Japan's Meiji era. It says something about the leadership of Kikkoman, according to Yotaro "Tony" Kobayashi, chairman and chief executive of Fuji Xerox, the Japanese partner of America's Xerox Corp. It is evidence of tradition and loyalty—qualities still highly regarded in Japan and Asia, even if many American corporate leaders seem to have given up on both.

Of course, one reason Kikkoman has managed to maintain tradition and cultivate loyalty may have something to do with its ownership. Even though Kikkoman is an independent company and is listed on the Tokyo and Osaka stock exchanges, a portion of the company is still owned by descendants of the founding families. Among the top 10 stockholders is the Sen Shu Sha (Long Life Corporation), basically a mutual financing association of family members, which owns 3.41 percent of the company shares. Among other things, the Sen Shu Sha operates Shimizu Park, a public park in Noda City, and maintains lands that for centuries have been the source of the wood used to make barrels and casks—the traditional shipping containers for soy sauce. The Bank of Tokyo-Mitsubishi, Ltd., Kikkoman's main bank, holds 2.89 percent of the corporate shares. That gives the company a pretty strong rudder as it rolls through the seas of commerce—both at home and abroad.

"There is something that certainly comes with tradition," said Kobayashi as he sat in his Tokyo office. "It's very difficult to quantify or explicitly explain what that is. But the tradition of quality and the quality of tradition are so prominent in a company like Kikkoman. It's a combination of the persistent quest of a high level of quality in its products and an attitude of total honesty in business dealings. It's an extremely fine characteristic."

Kobayashi and Fuji Xerox have more than a casual understanding of Kikkoman. In 1981, Fuji Xerox created a joint venture with Kikkoman called Chiba Xerox. After nearly 20 years of following Xerox's traditional system of direct marketing its copy machines, the Japanese joint venture company decided it could get its products into the Japanese marketplace more efficiently and less expensively by setting up a domestic system of joint marketing. Partner companies would be required to have products that had strong brand recognition, a good tradition of business, and successful distribution networks. The Kikkoman venture was one of Fuji Xerox's first joint distribution arrangements, and of the 30 such ventures it has in different prefectures of Japan, it is one of the company's most successful.

"The growth that has taken place in the past 16 years is remarkable," Kobayashi continued. "People in Chiba know Kikkoman...its tradition...and they know they are part of a joint venture with Fuji Xerox. Customers feel that if Kikkoman is the partner in this business, certainly it must be a good business and will have a long future."

But Kobayashi's relationship with Kikkoman began long before that joint venture. Both Kobayashi and Mogi are graduates of Tokyo's prestigious Keio University and both are among a select group of internationally minded Japanese business leaders who in the 1950s and 1960s came to America to study business. Today, with more than 80,000 Japanese students studying in American universities, that may not seem so unusual. But in the 1950s, with Japan still pulling itself out of the physical and emotional rubble of World War II, people like Kobayashi and Mogi were pioneers.

Kobayashi earned his MBA from Pennsylvania University's Wharton School in 1958, while Yuzaburo Mogi became the first Japanese to earn an MBA at Columbia University in 1961. But almost important as the advanced degrees they earned were the passionate views each held about the need for their companies to seek new international markets. Young business leaders like Mogi and Kobayashi belonged to a select group of individuals who possessed strong feelings about the important role international business would play in the growth of their companies in particular and Japan in general.

By the mid-1960s, the group's international personality was formalized when Japanese business leaders who had studied at Columbia, The Wharton School, Harvard,

Stanford, and the Massachusetts Institute of Technology began to gather for an annual alumni golf outing. Today, this group, which includes some of Japan's most powerful business leaders, still tees off once a year. And both Kobayashi and Mogi have served as cochairmen of the Japan American Cooperative Conference, a liaison organization between the Japanese Chamber of Commerce and Industry and the American Chamber of Commerce in Japan. Kobayashi was the first Japanese chairman and Mogi is its second.

While 35-year-old Fuji Xerox has none of the tradition of a company like Kikkoman, it has nevertheless managed to absorb some of that Kikkoman tradition through a kind of corporate osmosis. Aspects of the Mogi family creed can be seen in the way Kobayashi and Fuji Xerox approach business.

"I find the Mogi family extremely attractive," Kobayashi said. "There is a tradition there in the positive sense of the word. There are some companies that simply sit still on what they call tradition. But if you do that, tradition rots. That's not the case at Kikkoman. Soy sauce is probably among the most traditional household products in Japan, but Kikkoman took an early lead in taking that product international.

"That's a marvelous development," Kobayashi continued. "On one hand, it says something about the conservatism of a traditional company like Kikkoman, and on the other, it says something about the aggressiveness of its management. I think that's the real strength of Kikkoman—this blend of conservatism and its courage to take risks. I hope these are the same kinds of characteristics that are being recognized in Fuji Xerox."

Kenji Mizuguchi, founder and chief executive of Japan's Strategic Design Institute, which provides marketing strategy consulting for some of Japan's biggest companies, agrees.

"Many people think Kikkoman is a conservative company because its history is linked to a traditional product like shoyu," Mizuguchi said. "However, from a marketing standpoint, Kikkoman is not at all conservative. In fact, it's quite dynamic."

Nevertheless, Kikkoman is facing some challenges down the road. Kikkoman, adds Mizuguchi, is a company with two very strong points and one obvious weakness.

"One of its strengths is its brand equity, especially among Japanese housewives," Mizuguchi said. "The main reason for this is quality—a strong credential. The second strength is its distribution system. It has a well-entrenched nationwide distribution system. You can find Kikkoman products everywhere—even in tiny stores in the most remote parts of the country."

However, as strong as these points are, they have contributed to a soft spot in the Kikkoman armor, says Mizuguchi.

"Because of the long history and popularity of its brand as well as its vast distribution system, Kikkoman's sales force hasn't really had to push too hard," Mizuguchi pointed out. "I think Kikkoman has lost some opportunities because its sales force didn't work as hard as they could have."

Part of Kikkoman's problem is related to the big changes sweeping Japan's retailing market. For years, Japan's ubiquitous "mom and pop" shops were protected by the large retail store law which effectively banned stores larger than 500 m^2 from opening in a neighborhood without the approval of all the neighborhood's small merchants. That approval did not occur often. After all, what small merchants would gladly welcome a huge supermarket or department store in their own backyard? But a new wave of deregulation between 1990 and 1995—including revisions in the large retail store law—has facilitated the opening of more and more large outlets.

Japan's Economic Planning Agency estimates that this has generated some $34 billion more in consumption and another $8.5 billion more in capital investment. In 1988, for example, there were 1478 general supermarkets in Japan employing some 200,570 workers. In 1995, there were 1804 supermarkets employing 272,426 people.

Kikkoman has been slow to respond to this change in Japan's retailing environment, says Mizuguchi. Kikkoman's sales force tended to take care of its old-style mom and pop customers too well and the growing number of new supermarkets not well enough.

"Going into supermarkets is tough for traditional manufacturers like Kikkoman," Mizuguchi said. "Supermarkets started in the United States, where they have a lot of power and where they expect manufacturers to pay slotting allowances, a practice that is just starting in Japan."

Traditional manufacturers like Kikkoman have long used the nation's complex system of wholesalers to distribute its products, but Japan's new supermarkets want more direct sales from manufacturers and more retail support assistance, he adds. An example of that occurred in 1995 when Kikkoman competitor Ajinomoto and Japan's Daiei Supermarket chain announced an agreement for a low-price range of Ajinomoto food products. Kikkoman has not been as aggressive as it could be in areas such as this, says Mizuguchi.

In fact, Kikkoman has been reluctant to follow the pack in the Japanese food and beverage industry. While the trend toward low-price private brands is gaining momentum, Yuzaburo Mogi and his management team have decided to focus on Kikkoman's core business—a business geared, as Mogi stated in Kikkoman's 1995 annual report, "to providing healthy products that enhance the eating habits of consumers." To that end, Kikkoman has introduced its *Tokusen Marudaizu Shoyu* (Deluxe Soy Sauce) and *Tokusen Marudaizu Gen-en Shoyu* (Deluxe Low-Sodium Soy Sauce). It has also expanded its line of *Steak Shoyu* to include three varieties and has introduced a new concentrated soy sauce base called *Hon Tsuyu* that is used in making other soy sauce-based products.

Despite those efforts at product diversification, some insist that Kikkoman needs to further expand its product lineup both in Japan and abroad. For example, argues Mizuguchi, the company sells its soy sauce to hundreds of institutional customers who make soup and prepared foods. Kikkoman should be making those products itself, under its own brand name.

"Kikkoman is the company that pioneered the introduction of Oriental food and taste to the West," said Mizuguchi. "It needs to expand that role and introduce more products in the United States and Europe. With a bigger product lineup, Kikkoman can be a brand leader."

This is not new territory for Kikkoman, however. In addition to selling soy sauce to Americans, it has developed new products tailored specifically for American taste buds. Teriyaki Marinade & Sauce, for example, was introduced to American palates by Kikkoman more than 30 years ago. That was followed by Teriyaki Baste & Glaze and Teriyaki Baste & Glaze with Honey and Pineapple—neither of which are found in Japan. Kikkoman also introduced low-sodium Lite Soy Sauce, which has about 60 percent of the salt content of regular soy sauce.

While Kikkoman was the first Japanese soy sauce manufacturer to have a plant in the United States, it is not the only one. Yamasa, the number two brand in Japan, has built a 65,000-ft^2 plant in Salem, Oregon, that is producing about 1.7 million gal of soy sauce a year. Another Japanese company, San-J has built a plant in Virginia that is producing about 3000 kL (about 800,000 gal) per year.

Kikkoman is not sitting by idly, however. Its new plant in Folsom, California, will initially increase Kikkoman's U.S. manufacturing capacity by 2.6 million gal and help it maintain its hold on 50 percent of the U.S. soy sauce market, which is estimated to be about 40 million gal per year. That works out to about 17 oz of soy sauce per capita, compared with the 2.64 gal of soy sauce that each person in Japan consumes annually. Kikkoman marketing research shows that about 10 percent of the American population use more than one 12-oz bottle of soy sauce each month, while about half of all Americans use none. That presents some interesting scenarios for Kikkoman as it moves into the twenty-first century. For one thing, says Professor Kinugasa of Kanagawa University, sales should continue to climb in the United States."What will happen if U.S. sales become bigger than the Japanese market?" Professor Kinugasa mused. "Perhaps then Kikkoman's leadership will come from managers of the U.S. operations and not from those in Japan."

It's an interesting scenario for a traditional company like Kikkoman. Could an enterprise with its soul rooted so deeply in the Japanese experience find itself being led in the twenty-first century by someone whose background is 8000 mi away from Noda? While that may seem far-fetched today, it is no more inconceivable than someone suggesting in 1838—the year the Kikkoman brand name was registered with the Tokugawa Shogunate—that the company would someday be led by a member of the Mogi family who received a good portion of his education in New York.

As Professor Kinugasa points out: "The nationality of a company in today's global economy is not necessarily the basis for its international push. It's leadership."

Takeo Shiina, chairman of IBM Japan, another Keio University alumnus, agrees. Kikkoman is not one of Japan's largest 100 companies, Shiina points out, but it's one of its most international. The reason? Yuzaburo Mogi.

"Mogi is regarded in Japan as one of the most active representatives of Japanese business in the international arena," said Shiina, who puts Mogi into a category that includes Akio Morita of Sony and Yotaro "Tony" Kobayashi of Fuji Xerox.

Unfortunately, Shiina says, Japan has too few such international business leaders.

"Mogi is one of the few," Shiina said. "In fact, Japan's supposedly great global companies are really not very global at all. But Mogi and Kikkoman have a truly global view of business."

"Maurie" Kaoru Kobayashi, professor at Tokyo's Sanno Institute of Business Administration and Management and former Fulbright scholar at Manhattan College, takes that opinion a step further.

"Kikkoman should be a role model for any Japanese company that wants to go abroad and be accepted," Kobayashi said. "Kikkoman follows a slow and deliberate process when it enters a foreign market. It almost mirrors the fermentation process it uses in making shoyu. It takes longer, but you eventually end up with a much better product.

"It's more of an approach that a farmer might take. You have to sow the seeds, fertilize the crop, sometimes weather storms, and wait for the harvest. That's much different from a manufacturer who assembles a product. It's an attitude that shapes Kikkoman's long-term strategy."

4 CHAPTER

There's No Business Like Shoyu Business:

A Concise Soy Sauce Primer

Noda City is not a particularly remarkable place as far as Japanese towns go. There are none of the graceful Japanese castles that one finds in Himeji or Wakayama; no spectacular temples or shrines such as those in Kyoto or Nara; none of the glitter and glitz of Tokyo's Ginza or Osaka's Kita Shinchi. Situated between the Edo and Tone Rivers on the northwestern limb of Chiba Prefecture some 30 mi north of Tokyo, Noda is in fact a rather ascetic place replete with low-slung gray buildings and narrow winding streets flanked on either side by small shops, bland apartment complexes, and a few old wooden houses that hark back to the Meiji period. But then, that's what you would expect from a place that took root in the middle of soybean, wheat, and rice fields some 1100 years ago.

Noda is a city with a strong agrarian work ethic—a place where the faint fragrance of roasting wheat and soybeans permeates the air. Just as you notice the scent of hops and barley in the beer brewing districts of Milwaukee, Wisconsin, or the smell of corn being milled in Decatur, Illinois, the pleasant aroma of baking soybeans and roasting wheat wafts through the winding streets of Noda.

"There is something very natural about the aroma of roasting wheat and soybeans in the air," said Tetsuo Matsui, a former Noda-area resident now living in Minneapolis, Minnesota. "I grew up with it. It always reminds me of eating a bowl of my mother's *oden.* (Oden is a dish that consists of a variety of ingredients, including Japanese radishes, bean curd, potatoes, kelp, devil's tongue jelly, and yam cakes. As with many Japanese dishes, it depends heavily on soy sauce and a soy sauce-based stock for its unique flavor.)

Matsui, a retired chef in his early eighties who lives with his daughter in a Minneapolis suburb, pulled a 1-L plastic Kikkoman bottle from a shelf behind the grill of the small Japanese teppanyaki restaurant that his daughter and her husband operate.

"There is no other seasoning that is more important to Japanese cuisine," Matsui continued, rotating the bottle in his weathered brown hands. "Without shoyu, Japanese food and chefs like me would be lost. It is really the soul of the Japanese diet, and Noda is the mother of shoyu."

Dr. Shinichi Sugiyama, former managing director of Kikkoman's research and development division, takes that view a step further.

"Japanese cuisine virtually centers around soy sauce," he said. "It is as necessary to Japanese cooking as a motor is to an automobile."

Neither Matsui nor Sugiyama are exaggerating. Noda, a city of 110,000, is considered the fountainhead of Japanese shoyu. Many of its streets are lined with warehouses filled with soy sauce, and elevators containing soy sauce's two main ingredients (soybeans and wheat) tower over the town. It is here and in another town called Choshi on Cape Inubo, some 60 mi east of Tokyo, that the first barrels of what the world calls "soy sauce" were brewed in the early seventeenth century.

Today, Noda is headquarters of the Kikkoman Corporation, and it produces about 20 percent of all of Japan's soy sauce. The five Kikkoman manufacturing and bottling plants in Noda produce 1 million 1-L bottles of soy sauce every day. That is somehow appropriate considering that not far from Noda, in the town of Awagun, Japan's god of cooking and shoyu is enshrined in the Takabe Shinto Shrine. The god's name is Iwaka Mutsukari-no-mikoto, and he is worshiped by Japanese in the shoyu brewing and food-service industries.

According to local legend, Iwaka Mutsukari-no-mikoto was a servant of Japan's 12th Emperor Keiko (A.D. 71–130) and was elevated to the post of chief cook after preparing some exceptionally tasty clams for the emperor. He later oversaw the production of *miso* in the imperial court. Miso is a fermented soybean paste that is blended with different types of grains, including rice, wheat, and barley. It is considered the basic forerunner of shoyu and continues to be a fundamental seasoning in Japanese cooking.

Did Mutsukari-no-mikoto actually exist or is he simply a convenient icon conjured up by Japan's shoyu industry? Apparently, he really did exist. An ink portrait of him holding a clam in his right hand has survived the ages, and he is mentioned in ancient Japanese literature. With the spirit of the god of shoyu enshrined nearby, it seems appropriate that the first versions of modern shoyu should have originated in Noda.

It was in Noda that the Mogi and Takanashi families, the founders of today's Kikkoman Corporation, were among the first to add roasted and cracked wheat to a dark and thicker forerunner of soy sauce, which was made with soybeans and barley. This seasoning was a derivative of something called *hishio,* a semisolid seasoning with the consistency of porridge, that was made from soybeans and salt. Hishio was brought to Japan from China in the seventh or eighth century A.D., where it was known as *chiang* and had been in use since the Chou Dynasty (1100–256 B.C.) according to the *History of Soybeans and Soyfoods,* a book published by the California-based Soyfoods Center.

Tamari dates back to the thirteenth century when a Zen Buddhist priest named Kakushin returned from China's Temple of the Golden Mountain. While studying Zen at the temple, Kakushin learned how to make a sweet and chunky type of miso called *Kinzanji miso.* Miso, which along with shoyu is one of Japan's most important seasonings, is used in a variety of Japanese dishes from everyday *Miso-shiru* (Miso soup) to Japan's *Kaiseki-ryori,* or haute cuisine.

Kakushin, who returned to the Kokoku-ji Temple near the town of Yuasa in Wakayama Prefecture, not only taught the local Japanese about Buddhism, but he also taught them how to make Kinzanji miso. But Kakushin also experimented. He discovered that the liquid that settled at the bottom of the miso kegs during fermentation made a tasty seasoning and cooking liquid. By increasing the amount of water used to make miso, he could increase the amount of this excess liquid which he ran off or ladled out. The liquid was then used to flavor vegetables, fish, and tofu.

By the late 1300s, this liquid was being called *tamari,* a derivative of the Japanese verb *tamaru* which means "to accumulate." Early records show that the first *Yuasa shoyu* was sold commercially around A.D. 1290, and as it spread throughout Japan, it even inspired poets, who called the seasoning "deep purple." The seasoning's popularity was also helped by the civil wars that swept over feudal Japan during the Muromachi period (1328–1573). Soldiers carried shoyu from one battle to another, inadvertently introducing it to those who had never used it.

By the early 1500s, shoyu was being produced by farmers during slack periods in the agricultural cycle. Shoyu was made by combining cooked soybeans and roasted barley to form a dry mash called *koji.* Salt and water were then added to form a wet mash called *moromi* that was fermented for 75 days in open-top kegs. After 75 days, the mature moromi mixture was ladled into coarsely woven sacks and then pressed through them in order to extract the liquid tamari-shoyu. The dregs were then used as fertilizer or animal fodder.

The problem these early farmhouse tamari brewers had was in the pressing process. The cost of a sophisticated pressing machine that could be used to extract liquid from miso into a vat was far beyond what most farmers could afford. As a result, small family-run shoyu businesses began to evolve in Japan—especially in places like Noda and Choshi, which were blessed with warm and humid climates that are critical to the fermentation process and with a ready supply of wheat, soybeans, and salt.

In the 1630s and 1640s, these early brewers discovered they could lighten the heavy taste of the tamari-shoyu while enhancing its aroma by adding wheat and extending the fermentation time. In Choshi, other early brewers did the same—including the Yamasa and Higeta families, which still produce soy sauce.

These brewers also discovered that by roasting and cracking the wheat, they could dramatically improve the taste and aroma. The result was a brand new product that they called *shoyu* rather than tamari-shoyu.

The shoyu production process has undergone countless and significant modifications since those early days. Whereas it used to take a year or longer to produce brewed soy sauce, it now takes only about half that time. Sprawling, heavily automated factories with towering glass fiber fermentation tanks and computerized bottling lines have replaced the once quaint, labor-intensive shoyu breweries that helped transform Noda from a backwater on the road to Tokyo into the shoyu capital of the world.

Even though modernization and automation have improved the productivity of Kikkoman plants in Noda, the company nevertheless still uses some 100 wooden fermentation tanks that are about 70 years old. Kikkoman is a thoroughly modern company, but it's also obvious that tradition doesn't succumb easily. This is a company that takes pride in its history.

And Kikkoman's history in Noda is considerable. Not only is it Noda's biggest employer with some 1400 people working in seven manufacturing plants, a research and development facility, and a headquarters building, but it is also without a doubt Noda's biggest private benefactor.

In the early part of the twentieth century, Kikkoman built the city's waterworks. While that was not simply a civic gesture (after all, one of shoyu's most critical components is a supply of clean water), it was just the first of many such contributions Kikkoman would make to Noda over the years. For example, it built the city's library, cultural hall, railroad, museum, institute for scientific research, one of the city's fire stations, the community center, and an elementary school. In addition, Kikkoman built General Hospital and over the years has built almost 200 units of subsidized housing for its employees. Even some of the city's Shinto shrines and Buddhist temples were subsidized by Kikkoman. In 1975, the waterworks was turned over to the city government and over the years other facilities have been retired, but the company's involvement in Noda still runs deep. After all, Kikkoman—or at least the families who founded it—has lived in Noda for more than three centuries. It's a fact not lost on Noda City's leaders.

"Kikkoman Corporation has made great contributions to the city of Noda," said Takashi Nemoto, mayor of Noda City. "Several specific projects bear special mention. For example, the Brewers' Association, which was the former entity of Kikkoman Corporation, financed the launch of the Chiba Prefectural Railway Service, the present Noda Line of the Tobu Railway Company.

"Kikkoman also built the public water service in Noda City, which was the first in Chiba Prefecture," Nemoto added. "Kofu Hall, the recreational center for residents that was built in 1926 by Kikkoman Corporation, has been designated as a national cultural asset along with the Chiba prefectural government office of that era."

The company has even donated the former family estate of Saheiji Mogi—another national cultural asset—to the city, Nemoto points out.

"Kikkoman's role in laying the foundation of the city of Noda and its continued support of the city's development are recognized and appreciated," Nemoto said. "I ardently hope that the close relationship established with Kikkoman Corporation over the centuries will be continued in the future."

Nowhere is that long relationship more evident than in a unique museum devoted to soy sauce that was also financed by Kikkoman. The Noda City Museum contains more about soy sauce and its history than probably any other place in the world. Housed within the walls of a sprawling 200-year-old estate once owned by one of the original founding families of the Kikkoman Corporation, the museum's walls are lined with colorful eighteenth- and nineteenth-century woodblock prints showing the soy sauce production process. There are old blue ceramic and porcelain bottles that shoyu was once sold in. There are models of wooden *takasebune* flatboats that the forerunner of today's Kikkoman Corporation used to carry 18-L (4.75-gal) cedar kegs called *taru* from Noda to Tokyo on the Edo River. The boats, with their sails carrying the black Kikkoman tortoise shell logo that is still used by the company today, could make the trip from Noda to Tokyo in 1 day. With a population already exceeding 1 million in the seventeenth century, Tokyo was the largest city in the world, and it was an enormous market for shoyu.

While the growth of Tokyo spurred consumption of shoyu made in Noda, it was only a matter of time before Kikkoman and other soy sauce brewers began looking for more efficient ways to ship and package their product. By the late nineteenth and early twentieth century, the railroad had supplanted the takasebune flatboats, and by the 1930s, 4-L cans and 2-L glass bottles had begun to replace the cedar kegs that many shoyu manufacturers favored and still used until the mid-1960s.

Today, the kegs, which had a tendency to leak, are found only in museums like the one in Noda. Japanese consumers, who used to buy soy sauce in large glass bottles, now have a wide range of containers to choose from—from the large metal cans to the distinctive 5-oz clear glass bottle with the red plastic top that is as much a symbol of Kikkoman as its logo. The little soy sauce bottle with its twin spouts was introduced in 1961. The creation of industrial designer and Buddhist priest Kenji Ekuan, the bottle is considered a classic in the packaging industry.

"It has never changed in 30 years," Ekuan told the *Japan Times* on the occasion of the little bottle's 30th birthday.

"I've tried many times to improve it, but it was impossible. The original was perfect."

Ekuan worked more than a year trying to develop the bottle for Kikkoman. He tried some 200 different models before coming up with a container that has been likened to the classic green Coca-Cola bottle in its consumer appeal. The bottle is not difficult to spot on grocery shelves or on restaurant tables. Its red plastic top screws onto a thin neck that gradually expands into gently curving sides that widen at the bottom. More than 300 million of the reusable little bottles have been sold since 1961, according to Kikkoman's marketing division.

"That little Kikkoman bottle is to Noda what the Coca-Cola bottle is to Atlanta, Georgia," said a designer with GK Design, the worldwide design firm that Ekuan, now in his sixties, heads. "It's a masterpiece."

That view is shared by experts. In November 1997, the Glass Packaging Institute presented Kikkoman Foods, Inc., with its Packaged Food 1997 Clear Choice Award in recognition of its distinctive dispenser.

"The Kikkoman Soy Sauce dispenser combines practicality and functionality with a very creative design," said Joseph J. Cattaneo, executive vice president of GPI, a Washington D.C.-based trade association representing North American glass container manufacturers.

A tour of Noda leaves little doubt that you are in a kind of shoyu utopia. But in case some doubt still remained, you only need visit Goyogura, a complex of spotless white buildings with gabled black tiled roofs that sits along the banks of the Edo River. Goyogura resembles an Edo-period castle that looks as if it could have been built by the first Tokugawa shogun himself. A red wooden bridge arches gracefully over a moat that laps against the gray stone walls of the complex. At the front of the bridge stands a gnarled Japanese *sakura,* or cherry tree, while just behind, a wooded hill provides an emerald backdrop for the collection of buildings. In the middle is the *honmaru,* or center circle, with a *tenshu,* or tower, rising above the other buildings. It would be easy to assume that this maze of buildings is the Noda residence of the imperial family.

Actually, there is an imperial connection, but it has nothing to do with accommodations for the emperor. Inside these buildings, the ancient art of soy sauce brewing is practiced the way it was more than 300 years ago. Using the same type of tools, equipment, and methods, shoyu is made the old-fashioned way—with lots of time and tender loving care. Goyogura, however, is much more than simply a living museum. Built in 1939 by Kikkoman, it makes shoyu for Japan's imperial family just the way the Mogi and Takanashi families made it when they were licensed to produce soy sauce for the shogun in the early nineteenth century.

There are no glass fiber fermentation tanks here; no computerized control rooms; no bottling machines or other forms of twentieth-century manufacturing gadgetry. Instead there is a red brick wheat roaster, a small tiled culturing room, a wooden pressing machine, and 10 dark orange cedar vats in which a wet mash called *moromi* is stored for up to a year until it is removed and pressed through special cotton bags in order to extract the reddish-brown liquid we call soy sauce. Then it is pasteurized (a process that stabilizes the aroma and color), inspected, and put into special bottles destined for the *Kunaicho,* or imperial household. Goyogura produces 50 kL (13,200 gal) of shoyu each year with a portion sold to Japan's imperial family, according to Naoshi Tsukada, former manager of Kikkoman's Nakanodai plant just down the road.

Just as was the case when Kikkoman brand shoyu was bottled for the shogun, the process occurs under the watchful eye of a *Toji,* or brewmaster, who, along with other shoyu artisans, wear traditional eighteenth-century clothing. The Toji overseas workers with titles like *Mugi-iri* (wheat roaster), *Kamaya* (kettle tender), *Muromae* (koji maker), and *Moromi kaki* (moromi mash stirrer) as they toil in wooden rooms painted bright orange. Why orange? The color is significant because of its symbolic link to Shintoism, Japan's oldest religion. But orange was also used in the early nineteenth century to differentiate the soy sauce made for the shogun from that made for everybody else.

When Kikkoman built Goyogura to make soy sauce for the imperial family, the practice was continued. In the past, buildings used to produce shoyu were among the largest structures in Japan. In fact, they were rivaled only by Japan's major Buddhist temples—places like Todai-ji in Nara or Kiyomizu-dera in Kyoto. The reason? Most shoyu breweries housed dozens and, in some cases, hundreds of 8- to 15-ft deep fermentation tanks under one roof. Often, the tanks were 7 to 10 ft in diameter and held from 1500 to 3000 gal of wet mash.

The production method used to make soy sauce at Goyogura is perhaps the oldest, most historically authentic method in Japan. Goyogura soy sauce is made following a precise set of guidelines that dates back centuries. It's a process that still differentiates the soy sauce that is made by Kikkoman and the chemically produced product that many Americans and others outside of Japan may be familiar with.

The difference between naturally brewed soy sauce and the chemically produced variety is similar to the difference between a fine, naturally aged and fermented wine from France's Bordeaux or Burgundy region and the kind of wine that comes in bottles with screw-top lids.

There is no comparison. Just as you don't have to be a wine connoisseur to taste the difference between a fine 10-year-old wine and a $2 wine cooler bottled yesterday, you don't have to be an expert in Japanese cuisine to distinguish brewed soy sauce from one that is chemically produced. All you have to do is have someone put a little brewed soy sauce and the chemically produced variety in separate saucers. Even those with no or limited experience with soy sauce or Japanese cuisine will be able to tell which is which. Naturally brewed soy sauce is a delicate, almost transparent reddish-brown color. It possesses a unique bouquet that experts have concluded has nearly 300 different flavor components. Nonbrewed, chemically produced soy sauce, on the other hand, is usually a black opaque color with a harsh, overpowering flavor and an obvious chemical aroma.

Soy sauce is not intended to mask the flavor of the foods you put it on. It is not Dijon mustard or the pale green Japanese horseradish called *wasabi.* It is not meant to be used like ketchup or Worcestershire sauce, which tend to overpower or mask the flavor of foods they are used on. Soy sauce was created to enhance the flavors of meat, fish, and vegetables, not to hide them.

So why did shoyu develop in China and Japan, but not in Europe, with its rich tradition of fine cuisine? In his 1979 book *Searching for the Roots of Shoyu,* Kinichiro Sakaguchi, professor of fermentation science at Tokyo University, offers up some reasons.

First, few Westerners, he writes, ever learned how to make koji using molds such as aspergillus. Second, Europeans and Americans had no soybeans until the early twentieth century. And third, the basic ingredients that provide the delightful flavor of soy sauce and its good taste were unknown in the West.

While the general rule is to categorize soy sauce into brewed and nonbrewed varieties, fermented or brewed soy sauce can be further relegated to three basic types: Chinese light, Chinese dark, and Japanese shoyu.

Chinese light soy sauce is lighter in color than its Japanese cousin. While it is made from fermented soybeans, it contains no wheat and therefore has a less complex taste and more pungent flavor. It is used primarily for stir-frying, dipping, and as a table condiment.

Chinese dark soy sauce is not only darker than Chinese light soy sauce, but it is also thicker and sweeter. As with Chinese light soy sauce, it is made from fermented soybeans, but it also contains molasses. This type of soy sauce is most often used in Chinese stews and so-called red-cooking to add a deep vermillion color.

Japanese soy sauce is made with equal portions of fermented soybeans and wheat. It's the addition of wheat that accounts for the major difference between Chinese style brewed soy sauce and Japanese-style soy sauce. The wheat results in a soy sauce that has a much more delicate aroma and a richer, more balanced flavor than either Chinese light or dark soy sauce.

In Japan, Japanese soy sauce is further broken down into five officially recognized varieties under a 1970 set of criteria called the Japanese Agricultural Standards. First and most popular is *Koikuchi-shoyu,* or "deep color" soy sauce. This dark, reddish-brown soy sauce is the most traditional shoyu product and accounts for about 85 percent of all soy sauce sold in Japan.

Then there is *Usukuchi-shoyu,* or "light color" soy sauce, which is still produced in today's Hyogo Prefecture near the old imperial capital of Kyoto. This soy sauce, which has about a 13 percent market share, possesses a milder flavor than Koikuchi-shoyu and is used primarily in the Osaka-Kyoto area in soups, simmered dishes, and grilled foods.

Shiro-shoyu is a sherry-colored soy sauce that is used primarily in the Nagoya and Kyoto areas to enhance the taste of fish cakes, Japanese pickles, and various desserts. Its extremely light color is derived from using only two parts soybeans and eight parts wheat instead of equal amounts.

Saishikomi, or "kanro shoyu," is made like Koikuchi-shoyu, with one critical exception. Unpasteurized (raw) shoyu is used in place of brine to make the *moromi* wet mash. This results in a thick, dark brown soy sauce with a subtly sweet but stronger flavor than regular soy sauce. It is most often used on sushi and sashimi. This least used of Japan's soy sauces appears to have originated in the late eighteenth century in Yamaguchi Prefecture on the southwestern tip of Honshu, Japan's main island.

Finally, there is *Tamari.* This older ancestor of today's soy sauce is a thick, dark liquid that is a by-product of soybean paste production. Tamari is made from fermenting soybeans and little or no wheat. While it is similar to naturally brewed Japanese soy sauce, it is nevertheless darker and milder in flavor. Today it is used in Japan's foodservice and industrial food-processing industries. Japanese consumers, primarily in central Japan (Gifu, Mie, and Aichi Prefectures), use it as a dipping sauce for sashimi, for roasting Japanese rice crackers, and as a basting sauce for charcoal-grilled foods such as *yakitori* (skewered meat and vegetables).

Some 30 years ago, innovative variations of basic Koikuchi-shoyu were initiated by Kikkoman to meet new demands by Japanese consumers. A *gen-en,* or low-sodium soy sauce, was introduced that contained half the salt of traditional soy sauce. Originally made for hospitals and for those on salt-restricted diets, Kikkoman's "Lite" Low-Sodium Soy Sauce accounts for about 30 percent of Kikkoman's soy sauce sales in the United States.

Another variety of soy sauce produced by Kikkoman is *amakuchi,* a sweeter soy sauce flavored with licorice. There is also *ponzu,* a blend of soy sauce, citrus fruit juices, vinegar, and sweet sake. Other soy sauce-based products include Teriyaki, Sukiyaki, Oyster, Tempura, and steak sauce.

In mid-1997, Kikkoman added *Yakiniku-no-Tare,* to its lineup of more than 20 soy sauce-based products. Yakiniku-no-Tare is a new meat sauce designed for the Japanese market, and it comes in two flavors: a ruddy, Korean-barbecue style and a dark, lightly garlic-flavored Japanese-style.

While these soy sauces and their derivative cousins differ in taste, flavor, and consistency, they share one common attribute: They use Kikkoman Soy Sauce. Nonbrewed, chemically produced soy sauce, meanwhile, is a different story. Nonbrewed soy sauce has an opaque, dark brown color and a distinct salty taste. It is made by combining hydrolyzed vegetable protein with salt water, corn syrup, and artificial coloring. Soybeans are boiled with hydrochloric acid for 15 to 20 h. When the maximum amount of amino acid is removed from the soybeans, the mixture is cooled to stop the hydrolytic reaction. The amino acid is then neutralized, pressed through a filter, mixed with active carbon, and purified via filtration.

Eventually, color and flavor are introduced to the hydrolyzed vegetable protein mixture by adding varying amounts of caramel color, corn syrup for sweetness, and salt. The mixture is then refined and bottled. Sometimes the briny taste of chemically produced soy sauce is improved by using a lower concentration of hydrochloric acid with the soybeans. Then the mixture is fermented for a few days with salt-tolerant yeasts.

In either case, the end product takes only a few days to make. It is a much faster and less costly process than that used in creating naturally brewed soy sauce, yet soy sauces produced this way still retail for about the same price as the brewed variety.

However, speed kills. Specifically, the flavor and aroma of this type of soy sauce are simply not of the same quality as naturally brewed shoyu. There is a distinct chemical smell accompanied by a harsh, overpowering salty flavor. Naturally brewed and fermented soy sauce is one of the oldest biotechnology products known to humankind. It is not something that is accomplished overnight. As was the case 300 years ago, the production of naturally brewed shoyu follows a distinct three-step process: (1) *koji* production, (2) brine fermentation, and (3) refining.

Step 1 is to create the koji. Koji, a Japanese word meaning "bloom of the mold," is essential to the production of traditionally fermented or brewed foods. It is similar to the use of malt in the alcoholic fermentation of grains. Top quality soybeans and wheat, which are rich in protein and balanced with amino acids, are selected by passing them through a mesh screen. Both protein and amino acid are important in creating top-quality soy sauce. The beans and wheat are heated in special cookers that allow high-pressure cooking over a short period of time.

At this point in the process, Kikkoman introduces a proprietary koji mold culture and blends the wheat and soybean mixture with it. Just as Coca-Cola guards its recipe for its world-renowned soft drink, Kikkoman protects its mold culture from the elements, competitors, and other prying eyes.

But unlike Coca-Cola, which can always create copies of its recipes and store them in safe places, Kikkoman's proprietary microorganism is a living microorganism that dates back over the centuries. If something were to happen to it, it would be extremely difficult for Kikkoman to replicate all of the complex flavors and aromas found in its soy sauce. For that reason, the culture is safeguarded and managed with extreme care.

Once Kikkoman's proprietary microorganism is combined with the wheat and soybeans, the mixture is put into large, shallow, perforated vats where it is kept at a constant temperature. For the next 2 days, air that is kept at a precisely calculated temperature is circulated through the vats.

It's during this step that two critical enzymes are created as proprietary koji molds begin to grow within the koji dry mash mixture. The first enzyme causes the breakdown of protein into amino acids. This promotes soy sauce's good taste. The second enzyme transforms starch into sugar, which gives brewed soy sauce its subtle sweetness.

Step 2 begins when the resulting dry mash culture, or koji, is transferred to giant fermentation or brewing tanks where it is mixed with salt water to produce a wet mash called *moromi.* This is perhaps the most critical step in the process. The moromi must be allowed to ferment for several months in osmophilic lactic acid, bacteria, and yeasts. During this period, the soybeans and wheat are transformed into a semiliquid, reddish-brown "mature mash."

It's during this step that brewed soy sauce achieves its characteristic saltiness. This is also when the enzymatic reactions between the sugars and amino acids help develop the rich, clear color of brewed soy sauce. Brewed soy sauce's unique aroma is achieved because a special yeast begins to grow that changes some of the sugars to alcohol. At the same time, continuing fermentation transforms other parts of the sugars into acids that help create shoyu's aroma.

Step 3 begins following months of brewing in the giant moromi tanks. The raw soy sauce must be separated from the cakelike mash. To do this, the reddish-brown mature mash is pressed between layers of a special filtration cloth. The liquid that is expelled is then refined. Refining consists of separating the oil and lees from the prime shoyu, heat treating or pasteurizing the mixture, and then clarifying it by running it through special decanting tanks. Once this is done, it is bottled as finished soy sauce.

More than 300 years ago, when Kikkoman's proprietary koji mold culture was still in its formative years, the three-step process was essentially the same. However, the production facilities were a far cry from the sprawling, high-tech breweries of today. The ingredients were also much more motley.

When Shige Mogi (nee Maki) and her son Shichizaemon began making miso and shoyu in Noda in the 1600s, it was still very much a farmhouse industry. They were among thousands of small producers all over Japan who were using hundreds of different shoyu recipes that included varying proportions of ingredients. Sometimes shoyu makers used soybeans and barley; sometimes they used soybeans and wheat; and sometimes they used all three. There were also wide variations in the amount of water and salt used and in the fermentation time required to create farmhouse soy sauce.

It wasn't until the latter half of the Tokugawa period (1750–1868) that shoyu production began to assume a more standardized form. For beginners like the early Mogi and Takanashi families of Noda, there was a steep learning curve on the road to becoming accomplished shoyu producers. In many cases, they had to overcome three critical problems: First, they had to develop and learn a basic shoyu recipe. Second, they had to learn how to make koji and the starter koji mold. Third, they had to figure out a way to press the shoyu out of the moromi mash.

By the mid-1700s, several books were available in Japan that provided some guidance on shoyu production. These books and others produced in the nineteenth century reveal that shoyu making in eighteenth- and nineteenth-century Japan was still largely a cottage industry requiring fermentation times of anywhere from 15 to 30 months. In most cases, each family had its own secret recipe. When you consider that by 1890 Japanese records show that there were no fewer than 30,000 shoyu producers in the country, it's remarkable that Japanese shoyu has been consolidated into five distinct classes by the government.

Today, the number of shoyu producers in Japan has declined to about 2000. Along with a decline in the number of shoyu makers has come a decline in the per capita consumption of soy sauce in Japan. By the mideighteenth century, annual per capita consumption of soy sauce was about 4 L (about 1 gal). Considering that shoyu was still a condiment used mostly by Japan's upper classes during much of the Tokugawa era, that is significant.

By 1910, consumption had doubled to about 8 L (2 gal) and just before World War II hit an all-time peak of about 16 L (4.3 gal). Today, total soy sauce consumption in Japan stands at about 317 million gal per year. That works out to 10 L (2.5 gal) per person, and it appears to have leveled off in recent years. By comparison, annual soy sauce consumption in the United States is about 600 mL per person, or about 1.3 pt. While that may not seem like much, that's eight times more than it was when Kikkoman opened its first plant outside of Japan in Walworth, Wisconsin, 20 years ago.

The reason for the decline and flat consumption in Japan, according to marketing research conducted by Kikkoman, is continuing changes in the lifestyle of the Japanese people. Since the end of World War II—and particularly since the mid-1970s—Japanese eating habits have become, like the Japanese economy, much more global. For example, instead of eating a traditional Japanese breakfast that might include such dishes as raw eggs, *natto* (fermented soybeans), *nori* (dried seaweed), smoked fish, and rice, many of today's Japanese opt for ham, eggs, and hash-brown potatoes, which require salt and pepper rather than shoyu. Other Japanese stop off on the way to work for a breakfast sandwich at McDonald's or a couple of donuts and a cup of coffee at Mister Donut.

At the same time, Kikkoman research shows that almost 50 percent of Japanese wives now work out of the home. That means less time to prepare traditional Japanese-style meals which are labor-intensive and usually served in several courses accompanied by small dishes of soy sauce. Instead, they are opting for Western-style meals that can be served on a single plate at one time.

Yet another explanation can be found in the modernization of Japanese homes. Before World War II, few Japanese homes had electric refrigerators or freezers. That was still the case even into the 1960s. For centuries, food in Japan was often preserved by marinating it in soy sauce. At the same time, meat, fish, and vegetable dishes were often precooked by boiling them in soy sauce—another way of preserving food in Japan's humid climate. Today, with Japanese living in larger homes with more modern kitchens, there is no longer a need to use soy sauce as both a preservative and a seasoning. But there is little doubt that despite its lower per capita consumption, soy sauce continues to be the soul of Japanese cooking.

"It would be absolutely impossible to eat Japanese food without shoyu," said Miyoko Wagatsuma, a wife and mother who also works as a cook in her family's small *ramen* (Chinese noodle) shop in Tokyo's western suburbs. "It would be like trying to suck a bowl of ramen through a straw—it might be possible, but certainly not very enjoyable."

However, it's not just Japanese food such as ramen, *udon* (wheat flour noodles), or *nigirisushi* (raw fish on rice) that Wagatsuma uses shoyu on.

"I put it on hamburger and turkey, too," she said. "The Japanese diet may be very international today, but shoyu is like going home again."

5 CHAPTER

Diversify or Die:

Kikkoman's Strategies for Success

A reporter once asked former New York Mets manager Yogi Berra why fans were not coming out to the Mets games. Yogi's answer—now a classic bit of discombobulation—left the reporter scratching his head.

"If people don't want to come out to the ballpark, nobody's going to stop them," Yogi said.

We know what the sometimes bemusing Yogi meant. You can't make people do something they don't want to do.

Yogi could just as well have been talking about soy sauce consumption in Japan. You can't stop changes in eating habits. All you can do is adapt to them with new products. And that's exactly what Kikkoman has done. While it is still making the same top-quality shoyu it always has, soy sauce today accounts for less than 50 percent of Kikkoman's annual revenues. Thirty years ago, about 80 percent of Kikkoman's revenues were generated by soy sauce.

Today, about half of Kikkoman's revenues are generated by a broad range of products that includes a line of domestically produced fine wines, fruit and vegetable juices, and *shochu*, a traditional Japanese spirit.

The company also produces an extensive inventory of food-processing machinery, pharmaceutical products, and a line of more than 20 biotechnology products that includes diagnostic and industrial enzymes and substrates, and genetically engineered fruit and vegetables. In addition, it operates a chain of Japanese health clubs as well as several European and Japanese restaurants which it uses to promote sales of its soy sauce and wines.

As a result of this kind of diversification, some 26 percent of Kikkoman's sales and almost 50 percent of its profits are generated by its far-flung international operations. Some might think that a traditional Japanese company like Kikkoman, which has spent more than three centuries making a traditional Japanese product like shoyu, might be reluctant to enter new markets with new products. Kikkoman may be tradition rich, but it hasn't allowed tradition to become an anchor. In fact, if anything, the company is more aggressive since Yuzaburo Mogi became president and chief executive officer in 1995.

Not long after his appointment, Mogi created seven product managers in order to establish a stronger link between the consumer and Kikkoman's product development and production sectors. He also announced five basic policies and seven strategies that sent a bolt of electricity through the company. The first policy, Mogi said, would be to make Kikkoman a more aggressive company.

"We have to be more offensive than defensive," Mogi said, sitting in Kikkoman's corporate headquarters in Tokyo's Nishi-Shinbashi district. Mogi's words were interspersed between bites of fish, rice, Japanese pickles, and smoked meat that he lifted deftly from a lacquer *bento* (box lunch) with wooden chopsticks.

"Second, we have to speed up the process," he continued. "Shoyu is an old product with a long production cycle, but we have to speed that up so we are more responsive to customer needs. Third, we need to be more customer oriented. We think about wholesalers and retailers, but not enough about our customers—the people who buy our soy sauce and our other products."

Mogi stopped for a moment to scoop a bit of rice from his bento with his chopsticks.

"The fourth thing I want is for Kikkoman to become a company whose existence is appreciated by people," he said. "I want people to feel that Kikkoman's existence is somehow beneficial to their lives.

"Fifth and finally, to achieve these things, we must use group power. All affiliated companies within Kikkoman must work together, closely, and in harmony."

Sixty years ago, a goal that called on people at Kikkoman to work together may not have created many waves. But back then, 90 percent of Kikkoman's activities were centered around soy sauce. Things have changed dramatically at the company during the past 30 years. While there are no obvious divisions in the company, the concept of working together is more critical than ever at a time when the range of products it produces is broader than ever. In an era of reduced cycle times, greater customer demand, and global competition, Kikkoman's varying units and divisions must be more seamless in the development, production, and marketing of new products, say industry analysts.

"In the past, older generations of management were just happy to maintain the craftsmanship that goes into the production of soy sauce," said Yoshikuni Kato, a management consultant with A.T. Kearney in Tokyo. "But today, Kikkoman's younger generation of managers is much more aggressive.

"Kikkoman traditionally has been a modest company," Kato continued. "The mission has been to produce the best product for the market, but not really to advertise their strengths. I think people in top management want to be acknowledged by the market...to do something new and innovative that will move Kikkoman from its image of one of the most traditional companies in Japan to a company that is much more aggressive and innovative."

Indeed, the concept that Mogi and other top leaders are pushing through the ranks of the Kikkoman Corporation is this: You have to be a moving target. You cannot sit still and expect the market to pull you into the future. You have to be prepared to elbow your way to the front of the pack with products that will keep you moving forward. It's not an entirely new concept at Kikkoman. The company has been engaged in a long-term diversification program for more than 35 years. But with the company facing more competition at home and abroad, an aggressive strategy of innovation and diversification has never been more critical than it is today.

"As far back as 1960, the company realized the domestic market for its main product, soy sauce, was not expanding," Mogi said. "So we decided on an aggressive policy of *diversification* and *internationalization.*"

Kikkoman's top management saw that if the company was to survive, it would not only have to find a way to increase sales of its most traditional product (soy sauce) in new international markets such as the United States, Europe, and other parts of Asia, but it would have to develop new products for the Japanese market.

To promote and coordinate sales of its products in foreign markets, Kikkoman created an international business division in 1969. The path Kikkoman took toward diversification was highly innovative for a Japanese food company at the time and has provided today's leaders with a good model to follow.

In 1962, it created a wholly owned subsidiary called Mann's Wine Co. Ltd. (the name is derived from *manna,* the food from heaven described in the Bible, Exodus 16, and from the *man* in Kikkoman) and began producing wine from grapes it grew in the rich volcanic soil at the foot of fabled Mt. Fuji in Katsunuma, some 50 mi west of Tokyo. Using equipment imported from Germany and France, the Kikkoman subsidiary cultivated some of the finest merlot grapes outside of France and within a few years was bottling Japan's first domestically produced Western-style wine.

To Americans, this may not seem like such a novel idea for a company that had spent more than 300 years making a naturally fermented product like soy sauce. But Japan in the early and mid-1960s was a country almost totally unfamiliar with European red and white wines. In fact, most Japanese disliked the acidic flavor of fine French Bordeaux and Burgundy wines. A few sweet German Spaetlese and Auslese wines were about the only wines Japanese consumers seemed to like. In 1965, only about 100,000 gal of Western wine were consumed in Japan, recalls Asao Kawamura, former deputy general manager of the Mann's marketing division. That works out to less than a tablespoon for every Japanese.

Kikkoman's marketing strategy was not to try to convince Japanese consumers that they really should like Western wines. Instead, Kikkoman took a different track. It promoted Western wine as a kind of healthy alcoholic beverage. Western wine's acidic, alkaline character would actually be beneficial to hardworking Japanese businessmen and women who suffered from "tired blood," according to Kikkoman's marketing campaign. In an effort to convince the nation's hardworking "salarymen" that they should be drinking Western-style wine with their meals rather than beer and sake, Kikkoman set up tasting booths on the streets of Tokyo's busy Otemachi and Marunouchi business districts. Kikkoman sales personnel offered samples of wine to harried Japanese businesspeople, and soon many began drinking wine with their meals. Some Japanese marketing experts credit Kikkoman with helping to create one of Japan's first wine booms.

Once Kikkoman had stimulated demand for its wine, it turned its attention to working on new distribution channels. In the late 1960s, most Western-style wine was available only in restaurants and hotels. Consumers couldn't find it in liquor stores or supermarkets, both of which carried Kikkoman's lineup of shoyu. But if liquor stores and supermarkets could carry soy sauce, which has about a 2 percent alcohol content, they could also carry wine, reasoned Kikkoman's marketing strategists. Not long after its unique outdoor one-on-one marketing campaign, Kikkoman began to push its wine into liquor stores by using tasting demonstrations with customers.

Once store owners saw customers lining up to get free samples of Mann's wines, it wasn't too difficult to convince them to stock the product on their shelves. By the late 1960s, say Japanese marketing experts, Kikkoman, still using its one-on-one marketing techniques, had pushed the home wine-drinking market from virtually nothing to almost 20 percent of wine consumption in Japan.

In 1970, with the World Expo in Osaka pulling in millions of Japanese who were flush with discretionary income and eager to be as "Western" as possible, Kikkoman began recrafting its Mann's Wine marketing strategy. Instead of pushing wine as a healthy drink, it would promote it as Japan's new social drink—a drink that implied status and sophistication."At the Osaka Expo, about 240,000 people visited Kikkoman's restaurant," recalled Kawamura. "We offered set meals and served red wine for meat dishes and white wine for fish and poultry dishes."

It worked. With more and more Japanese traveling abroad on business and on holidays, palates were becoming more and more sophisticated. By 1972, Kikkoman had launched a $20-million national Mann's Wine advertising campaign. Ads were everywhere—in newspapers, on television, radio, and in subway cars. And they carried a message that was unusual for a Japan in which many men still believed women should walk three paces behind them when in public. The message was this: Wine is not a drink meant to be enjoyed alone. Men and women should drink it together at home, in restaurants, or on any special occasion. To emphasize its point, Kikkoman launched a slogan that said: "Drink wine with your spouse!" The campaign used one of Japan's top Kabuki actors and his wife and showed them drinking wine together at home over dinner.

Nevertheless, it was a campaign that insisted Japan was moving toward a new lifestyle—one in which husbands and wives in particular and men and women in general should behave more as partners, rather than as "master-servant." With more and more women already beginning to work outside of the home and others opting to become more involved in politics, social issues, adult education, and consumer affairs, Kikkoman's marketing campaign was right on target—again.

"We increased wine consumption in Japan about sevenfold in a 20-year period from 1973 to 1993," said Sadao Yoshida, executive managing director of Kikkoman's marketing division. "We identified a new trend, a new Western lifestyle, and we used our centuries-old knowledge of biotechnology and fermentation to make some of the first Western-style wine in Japan."

In 1964, the Mann's winery produced 26,000 gal of wine. Today, its annual production of 2.6 mil gallons is almost 100 times higher, and it has a 10 percent market share of the Japanese-made wine market. It is also the largest of the Katsunuma region's 87 wineries.

While Kikkoman would like to have a larger share, it refuses to sacrifice quality in order to increase production. In the past, and even today, much of the "Japanese" wine sold in Japan was a blend of domestically produced and bulk imported wines. A large part of Mann's total production, for example, are wines blended with bulk wines from Europe and South America. One reason for this is the difficulty vintners have with growing grapes in Japan's rainy climate, which receives nearly two times as much rain each year as France's Bordeaux district. Excessive rainfall during the fall makes it difficult to time the harvest, says Nobuhiko Matsumoto, head of Mann's quality control division. If you harvest the grapes too soon to beat the fall rains, they are not ready. If you wait until mid- or late-October, the grapes are already rotting on the vine.

Kikkoman has overcome this problem, however. In 1982, it began using an ingenious retractable roof designed by Mann's employees that protects the grapes from excessive rain. Called the Mann's rain-cut system (MRCS), the device consists of a metal trellis that spans the grapevines. The trellis is covered with a fine mesh which can be raised or lowered as needed. The mesh allows sunshine and air to hit the grapes, but it also allows vintners to control the amount of rain that falls onto them.

After a few growing seasons, the vintners at Mann's discovered a side benefit to the rain-cut system. The amount of the grape crop damaged by the elements decreased.

Before the MRCS was installed, only about 45 percent of the black, russet, and green grapes came through a season undamaged. Today, 95 percent of the grapes grown by Mann's are healthy.

But that's not all the MRCS has done for the grapes grown by Mann's. Because the grapes can remain on the vine until they are fully ripe, their sugar content has increased 20 percent. At the same time, because the rain-cut system effectively controls the environment, Mann's is required to use less chemical fertilizers—a fact that results in a more natural product.

Most important, however, is that Mann's has the technology and know-how today to cultivate the kind of domestically grown grapes that have resulted in an array of distinctly Japanese wines, sparkling wines, and brandy—something unheard of just 20 years ago.

In 1963, barely a year after establishing Mann's Wine, Kikkoman continued its march toward greater diversification when it launched a subsidiary called Kikko Foods Corporation, whose business was to pack and distribute a wide range of branded foreign products for the Japanese market. Research by Kikkoman confirmed that Japan's changing eating habits were much more than a postwar fad. Japanese consumers actually liked certain Western foods—among them, tomato-based foods. Kikkoman was sure it could sell products such as tomato juice and ketchup through the same sales network it used for soy sauce.

The company quickly signed a licensing agreement with America's Del Monte Corporation that allowed Kikkoman to produce Del Monte tomato juice and ketchup for the Japanese market. In 1990, it signed a perpetual rights agreement with Del Monte giving it exclusive rights to produce, package, and sell Del Monte brand products in Asia, except for the Philippines. Not long thereafter Kikko Foods Corporation was renamed Nippon Del Monte Corporation.

Kikkoman's link-up with Del Monte was a major coup. Del Monte, founded in California in 1892, was considered the Rolls Royce of the U.S. packaged food industry. With annual revenues of $1.2 billion, Del Monte is

America's largest branded maker and distributor of canned fruits and vegetables. Its corn, green beans, peas, tomatoes, peaches, pears, and other products are purchased from more than 2500 independent growers.

"Del Monte had already done a good job of penetrating the Japanese market with its premium brand of canned vegetables," recalled Kiyochika Fukushima, former general manager of the marketing and merchandising department. "With Western food becoming more and more popular in Japan in the 1950s and 1960s, Kikkoman's leaders felt that a top-quality product like Del Monte would help establish Kikkoman as a modern Westernized company in the minds of Japanese consumers," added Fukushima, who is currently general manager of logistics of Kikkoman Corporation.

Kikkoman's strategy was not to flood the Japanese market with the same Del Monte products that sold well in the United States, but to pick its spots with unique products tailored for the Japanese palate. Among other things, it decided to focus on the high end of the market with quality products. Tomato-based products like tomato juice and ketchup were a good choice. Both were relatively new to Japan, but it was obvious that Japanese consumers liked both.

The first tomato didn't find its way to Japan until the 1870s. But by 1903, as many as 25 different varieties had been introduced from the United States alone. Of those, the tomato that was the most popular and which continues to be the most popular in Japan is the slightly pinkish Ponderosa, which in Japan is known as the *Momotaro.*

Ten years after Kikkoman began marketing Del Monte products in Japan through the same sales and distribution network it uses for soy sauce, it had gained 30 percent of the Japanese market for tomato products and has become a formidable competitor to Kagome Co. Ltd., the Nagoya-based company that is Japan's largest producer of tomato processed foods. Just as it helped push domestic sales of Western-style wine to new heights, Kikkoman's aggressive marketing of Del Monte products since the 1960s has helped move per capita consumption of tomato juice in Japan to three times that of the United States.

By 1990, Kikkoman had expanded its licensing agreement with Del Monte. Instead of marketing only tomato-based products such as tomato juice and ketchup, Kikkoman acquired the perpetual right to the Del Monte brand name in Japan, Oceania, and the rest of Asia, with the exception of the Philippines. It was a hefty investment for Kikkoman. To acquire those perpetual marketing rights, Kikkoman had to shell out $110 million. In addition, it has another $38-million investment in Del Monte itself, $25 million of which is directly with Del Monte Corporation in the United States. In 1997, Del Monte Foods Co. was acquired by the investment firm Texas Pacific Group, which announced plans to revitalize both management and the Del Monte brand name.

"The bottom line is, the brand is a wonderful brand, but [unlike the Japanese-owned subsidiary] the U.S. company literally has no resources to build value-added products," said David Stone, a partner at New England Consulting Group, a consumer marketing firm.

Revitalization is not a problem at Nippon Del Monte, however. On the contrary, industry analysts consider it a leader in Japan's packaged foods industry.

"The great strength of Kikkoman is its wonderful mix of tradition and innovativeness," said A.T. Kearney's Kato. "The company may look slow in making decisions, but once consensus is reached, it can move very fast."

Today Kikkoman markets a broad range of products that includes fruit juices, canned fruit, tomato-based seasonings, and canned vegetables.

"Most Japanese fruit juices are made from concentrates, but Del Monte uses fresh fruit in some of its drinks," said Fukushima. "We get fresh pineapple shipments from the Philippines weekly. Usually ketchup is made from tomato paste, but we make some of our ketchup from freshly harvested tomatoes in the summer—hence the product name Summer Harvest."

Kikkoman's Del Monte brand products such as tomato juice and ketchup are produced at four Japanese plants which employ some 400 people. The largest of these is a sprawling facility in Numata, a town of 47,000, some 70 mi northwest of Tokyo in Gunma Prefecture. Numata is nestled in the foothills near Mt. Tanigawa, a popular ski and winter sports resort area. Before Kikkoman built the Nippon Del Monte plant on the edge of Numata, the chief product in the town was lumber. Today, stretching out beyond the town are scores of fields dedicated to tomato cultivation. It's here, in these fields, that the company has developed several new varieties of tomatoes, including the NDM051, a variety created specifically for machine harvesting. The NDM051, which was introduced in 1990, is the result of more than 10 years of research by Nippon Del Monte's staff of researchers, plant biologists, and geneticists. The new tomato, which is used almost exclusively for juice, has a much thicker skin than regular tomatoes, explained Eiji Ishimura, a senior researcher in Nippon Del Monte's research and development division. It also has a "jointless" stem.

"The thicker skin allows the tomato to grow on the ground rather than on trellises," said Ishimura. "That means the tomato can be harvested by machine, rather than by hand. The jointless stem means that the entire stem snaps off cleanly at the time of picking, thus making the tomatoes ready for processing as soon as they leave the field."

The NDM051 tomato can also remain on the ground for long periods without spoiling. That allows farmers to harvest all their tomatoes at the same time, rather than five or six times each year as they did in the past, explains Ishimura. Why is this important? For one thing, says Ishimura, it means Nippon Del Monte can produce tomato juice much less expensively than before.

"It used to take 360 people to harvest 1 ha per season (about 2.5 acres) of tomatoes," said Ishimura. "Now, because of the NDM051 tomato, we only need about 70 people per hectare. There is no doubt that our biggest breakthrough to date has been the unjointed stem."

But Nippon Del Monte's search for a better tomato hasn't stopped with the NDM051 variety. Less than a 5-minute walk from Ishimura's office are four greenhouses replete with some 2000 experimental and hybrid tomato plants. Ishimura and his three researchers are breeding each plant in the four hothouses for a certain set of traits. Eventually, says Ishimura, after the plant's genes are stabilized—a process that takes six or eight generations—the plants will be cultivated for their seeds, and new varieties and hybrids will be used.

"We develop 500 new varieties every year and then select two or three for regional trials," Ishimura said. "Our chief concern is quality. The essential factors for tomato juice are color, taste, and aroma. Tomato juice must look appetizing and there must be a correct balance between the sweet and sour taste of the juice."

But there is something else that Ishimura and his research team are working on in addition to a better tasting, better looking, better smelling tomato: a healthier tomato. Every year, about 20 percent of Japan's tomato crop is damaged by a deadly virus called the cucumber mosaic virus (CMV). The disease, which is spread by centimeter-long aphids, curls the tomato plant's leaves and withers the fruit and stems.

Back in 1984, Dr. Haruki Sayama and a group of Nippon Del Monte researchers began working on a long-range project whose goal was to find a way of controlling the cucumber mosaic virus without the use of pesticides. It was a formidable challenge, but today, Dr. Sayama and his team have achieved a startling string of successes that could have broad implications for the international tomato growing industry.

Until now, the only way farmers could deal with CMV was by applying insecticides or by covering all their tomato plants with cheesecloth nets designed to prevent aphids from accessing the plants. Using pesticides is not only expensive, but it's an environmentally unfriendly way to deal with the problem. And the cheesecloth nets are only marginally effective.

Now there is another, more effective alternative. Dr. Sayama and his team have developed a vaccine for tomato plants. It's an original solution that has grabbed the attention of plant pathologists and agronomists the world over. In essence, the solution developed by Dr. Sayama's team is a system in which each plant is "inoculated" against CMV. While that may conjure up an image of white-coated scientists using a syringe to inject each plant with a vaccine, the process is quite different.

"We spray young tomato seedlings with attenuated CMV in a buffer solution," explains Dr. Sayama. "Then a tiny roller is used to `wound' the plant tissue, thereby allowing the vaccine to penetrate the plant."

This so-called spray-roller method of inoculating tomato plants has been so successful that Nippon Del Monte has introduced three new inoculated tomato plant varieties that are resistant to CMV: Vitamin Ace (an orange tomato hybrid with six times more betacarotene and two times more vitamin C than other tomatoes); Summer Kiss (a plant with large fruit which is also resistant to the tobacco mosaic virus); and Twinkle (an extremely sweet cherry tomato hybrid with three times the vitamin C content of other cherry tomatoes).

In 1994, Nippon Del Monte test marketed 5700 inoculated tomato seedlings at garden centers throughout Japan. Even though the plants cost three times more than regular tomato plants, consumers snapped them up. In 1997, some 800,000 plants used for juice and another 400,000 fresh market tomatoes were inoculated with attenuated CMV vaccine.

Because Kikkoman has been on the leading edge of this type of research, Dr. Sayama and his team have collaborated with both Japanese and international universities and institutes, exchanging genetic maps and DNA markers in an effort to speed up the breeding process. This has moved Dr. Sayama and Nippon Del Monte into the direction of creating transgenic tomato plants, which carry the CMV resistance factor in their genes. Interest in the vaccine itself has come from melon and bell pepper growers, as well as nurseries and florists.

While tomato juice and ketchup remain Nippon Del Monte's best-selling products with more than 70 percent of the company's sales, Yuzaburo Mogi has challenged the company to come up with new products. To that end, Nippon Del Monte researchers like Chikara Katano, who heads the company's product development division, are busy working on a lineup of more than 20 new products, including a carrot ketchup product.

"We are under pressure to create new products that will further strengthen Nippon Del Monte's brand position," said Shinichi Sugiyama, president of Nippon Del Monte Corp.

In order to concentrate on that goal, Kikkoman has canceled contracts to produce and bottle Lea & Perrins Worcestershire sauce, Ocean Spray cranberry products, and Ragu spaghetti sauces and pizza sauces. The company has also developed a line of upscale food products that are marketed in Japan under the Hotel Del Monte brand name. The name is taken from a stately old Monterey, California, hotel. The line includes French onion and corn soups, marmalade, canned vegetables, and various tomato products.

However, the newest product coming off Nippon Del Monte's Numata bottling lines at the rate of 80,000 cases a month in early 1997 was something developed in Noda by Kikkoman's soy sauce research and development facility. Called *Yakiniku-no-Tare,* this new meat sauce designed specifically for the Japanese market was launched with some of the biggest publicity in Kikkoman's recent history.

Hideki Matsui, a center fielder for the Yomiuri Giants and one of Japan's top baseball players, was recruited to endorse the sauce, which comes in two flavors: a reddish-brown Korean-barbecue type of sauce called *Aka Dare* (red sauce) and a dark, lightly garlic-flavored Japanese-style sauce called *Kuro Dare* (dark sauce). Signing Matsui to endorse its Yakiniku-no-Tare was considered a major coup for Kikkoman in the world of Japanese marketing because it was the first advertising campaign Matsui had ever agreed to become involved in. In 1996, Matsui was named Most Valuable Player in Japan's Central League.

Both *Aka Dare* and *Kuro Dare* (in Japanese, the *T* sound changes to a *D* sound following a vowel) are meant to take advantage of the increasing popularity of red meat in the Japanese diet. Beef imports have skyrocketed since Japan's restrictions on beef imports were liberalized in the early 1990s. In 1995, according to the Japan External Trade Organization, Japanese consumed an average of 30 kg (66 lb) of beef and pork per person. A decade ago, the figure was half that.

Those who have experienced Korean barbecue dishes such as *kalbi* or *bulgogi* will be familiar with Aka Dare. Among other ingredients, the 350-mL plastic container with the red label contains a Japanese miso base, soy sauce, tomato paste, garlic, sesame oil, onion chips, and red pepper.

Kuro Dare, meanwhile, which comes in a 350-mL plastic bottle wrapped in a black label, contains a soy sauce base, sugar, orange juice, minced apple, garlic, scallions, honey, vinegar, onion chips, red pepper, Korean miso, and lemon.

"Normally, we take about 1 year to develop a product, but with this product, we didn't want to make any mistakes," said Kunitomo Kidzu, who headed the research and development team in Noda that came up with the new products. "We spent 2 years developing Yakiniku-no-Tare. We wanted to be sure this product would be a success."

Kidzu and his group, which included a research team of three women and one man, created and tested several formulas before deciding on those used in both products.

"When we tested the final formula for both Yakiniku-no-Tare products on focus groups, they received the highest score of all the products Kikkoman has ever produced," said Kidzu.

That's good news because Yakiniku-no-Tare is one of those products that Yuzaburo Mogi has included in the series of strategies he announced when he became president and CEO in 1995. Of those, Mogi says that the first four are short range, the next two are medium range, and the last is long range.

The first strategy, says Mogi, is to do something about the decline in domestic consumer demand for soy sauce.

"We have to revitalize the soy sauce business," Mogi said. "With per capita consumption of soy sauce declining in Japan, we have to create more high value-added products such as Tokusen Marudaizu or Deluxe Soy Sauce that is made from special soybeans and other ingredients selected for their purity."

Kikkoman is creating new products for Japan's industrial soy sauce customers to meet vigorous competition. These new products are for specialized uses and are less expensive.

The second strategy, Mogi adds, is to create new shoyu-related products such as bases for noodle soups and sauces that will allow Japan's increasingly active housewives to create meals faster by cutting down on cooking times. For example, a new *Hon Tsuyu,* a concentrated soy sauce base used by general consumers, and three new varieties of *Steak Shoyu* were introduced a year before Yakiniku-no-Tare made its debut—all part of Mogi's plan to provide new products for new lifestyles.

The third strategy is to make the Kikkoman brand better known globally while expanding overseas business. That is reflected in the company's two newest foreign manufacturing ventures: the new plant in the Netherlands, which was formally opened October 10, 1997, and the new Folsom, California, facility that Kikkoman broke ground for in March 1997.

"We have grown in North America," Mogi said. "But we haven't introduced any new big products in the U.S. market since the 1960s when we brought out teriyaki sauce."

That's why the Kikkoman marketing and planning unit was moved from San Francisco to Chicago in April 1997. The unit will be responsible for coordinating new product development between Kikkoman Foods, Inc. (the subsidiary which oversees Kikkoman's Walworth, Wisconsin, plant) and Kikkoman International, Inc. (the company's San Francisco-based marketing arm). The objective, said Mogi, is to promote better communications with the Walworth production facility and to speed up development of new products for the U.S. market.

The fourth short-term strategy is to change the old company's climate or traditional orientation. "Kikkoman,"

Mogi insists, "must be strong and challenging, aggressive and muscular.

"Each employee has to be more dynamic and reach to his or her full ability," Mogi continued. "Without changes in the company climate, Kikkoman cannot grow in the global market and, indeed, might not even survive in the Japanese market.

"If we are to be winners in the next century, we will need more innovative behavior," warned Mogi. "We will have to be more offensive minded. We will have to change our character to become even more aggressive and innovative than we already are. That is our challenge."

For the medium term, Mogi would like to see some new Del Monte brand products that would spur sales. Under development by Nippon Del Monte are several Chinese-style garlic, chili, and oyster sauces; new chicken and corn potage soups; and a new Fruits Salad drink that is a unique combination of several fruits and vegetables.

Another medium-term strategy laid out by Mogi calls for the company to create a new kind of liquor or alcohol-based product. The company already produces *shochu,* a clear Japanese spirit, and *mirin,* a sweet sake used in Japanese cooking, under its Manjo brand label. Mirin, especially, has an opportunity to grow because deregulation had made it easier for supermarkets to carry the sweet sake. Mogi also wants to push Mann's Wine to come up with some new products, particularly in the late 1990s when a new wine boom appeared to be in progress in Japan.

For the long term, Mogi and Kikkoman are betting on biotechnology, which is a natural for Kikkoman. Soy sauce, after all, is one of humankind's oldest—if not *the* oldest—commercial biotechnology products.

"We need to develop new products from the biotechnology sector and we need to do it as quickly as possible," said Mogi. "Our investment in this area is growing."

Once again, Kikkoman is no stranger to the world of biotech. More than 30 years ago, it developed biotech products such as Molsin, an acid-stable protease, and Stalese, an acid-stable amylese, that are sold to pharmaceutical companies as aids for digestion. Kikkoman researchers have also developed a food safety testing kit as well as enzymes for clinical diagnostic uses and for the industrial production of gallic acid, which is used in the production of pharmaceuticals and semiconductors.

6 CHAPTER

The Road to Walworth:

Kikkoman's Big Gamble on the Big Foot Prairie

Within easy driving distance of both Chicago and Milwaukee, in the rolling hills of southern Wisconsin, is a collection of those intriguing little places that make trivia zealots drool. For example, in Appleton, there is the Houdini Historical Center, which houses the personal effects, leg irons, handcuffs, and lock picks used by Appleton's favorite son, the legendary Harry Houdini. In Burlington, there is the Spinning Top Exploratory Museum, a hands-on place where more than 1000 antique tops, yo-yos, and gyroscopes are displayed and demonstrated. There is also the Mount Horeb Mustard Museum, which boasts the world's largest collection of mustard—some 2300 different varieties at last count.

Then there is Walworth, the soy sauce capital of America and the Western hemisphere. Walworth has claimed that title since 1973 when the Kikkoman Corporation opened the doors of its 500,000-ft^2 factory with the capacity to turn out 9000 kL (2.4 million gal) of soy sauce that first year.

However, there is another even more impressive bit of trivia about Walworth that few Americans (or Japanese, for that matter) may be aware of. The Kikkoman Soy Sauce plant is generally conceded to be the first full-blown Japanese manufacturing facility ever constructed in the United States, according to sources in the U.S. Department of Commerce. While it's true that Japan's Sony Corp. opened a television picture tube assembly plant that it had previously purchased near San Diego in 1972, it wasn't producing a product from scratch the way Kikkoman's Walworth plant was. Nor was it producing a 100 percent Japanese product like brewed soy sauce.

Add to all that the fact that in this stronghold of milk and cheese only a handful of Walworthians back then could tell the difference between soy sauce and India ink and you have a rather remarkable collection of historical minutiae.

Walworth, after all, sits on the southern part of the Big Foot Prairie in Walworth County, which local historians are quick to point out is the only perfectly square county in the United States. In the midseventeenth century, the area now occupied by Kikkoman's 200-acre plant was Potawatomi Indian turf. The Potawatomis were an Algonquin tribe that moved into what is now southern Wisconsin from Michigan around 1640—at about the time the first generations of the Mogi family were learning to make what the world today calls soy sauce in Noda, some 8000 mi away.

But by 1837, about the same time that the Kikkoman brand was given trademark status by Japan's Tokugawa shogun, things were changing fast for the Potawatomis. Chief Mauck Suck (Big Foot), the last Potawatomi chief to reign in Wisconsin, had just signed over Native American lands known today as the Big Foot Prairie to the U.S. government and was on his way (reluctantly) to Kansas with the rest of Wisconsin's Potawatomis. A few months after Chief Big Foot's departure, the U.S. government began selling some of the richest farmland in America for $1.25 per acre.

According to Walworth Village president and local attorney Dave Rasmussen, who is a one-man repository of local Walworth history and lore, in the spring of 1837 Christopher Douglass dropped his plow into the rich black soil that abounds in the Big Foot Prairie and plowed a furrow 2.5 mi long to mark one boundary of his land. Two years later, the town of Walworth was formed and the first schoolhouse was built.

By 1842, the area's first tavern—known as Douglass Corners—was opened not far from what is now the Kikkoman factory. While the temperate Yankee Baptists from New England who settled the rich farmlands around Walworth and helped found Walworth were not exactly enthralled by Douglass Corners, it was a sign of the times. Not more than 35 mi to the east, the bustling community of Milwaukee was being settled by German immigrants, many of whom would use the technology and know-how they brought from Europe to create Milwaukee's beer-brewing industry.

While beer was just beginning to make Milwaukee famous in the early nineteenth century, the founders of today's Kikkoman Corporation had already turned Noda into the shoyu capital of the planet. As with Milwaukee's beer brewers in the nineteenth century, these were heady days for Japan's shoyu brewers. Demand for soy sauce was steadily increasing year by year and it was all the Noda brewers could do to keep up. New technologies were adapted that allowed the industry to shorten production time; new, more efficient distribution channels were created, and the quality of soy sauce was improving steadily.

That's the way things remained for Japan's soy sauce industry until the mid-1950s when Japan's growing appetite for Western foods began to have a significant impact on the consumption of traditional fare such as fish and rice, both of which are often eaten in meals in which soy sauce plays a prominent role.

In 1965, according to a 1996 report called *Food and Agriculture in Japan*, published by the Foreign Press Center of Japan, about 1200 cal of the average daily caloric intake of 2500 cal came from rice. That was not only a 10 percent decline from a decade before, but it was a harbinger of things to come—and Kikkoman knew it. For example, in 1996, rice accounted for just 600 cal in a daily diet that had grown to 2627 cal. Rice consumption has fallen by 50 percent in the past 30 years in Japan, and it is continuing to fall rapidly.

Another report issued in 1997 by Japan's Management and Coordination Agency confirmed this trend. A preference for domestic and imported beef has eroded the consumption of fish, and a predilection for pasta, potatoes, bread, and other baked goods reduced rice consumption from about 120 kg (about 265 lb) to 98 kg (216 lb) per household between 1993 and 1996—a drop of almost 15 percent.

With less rice and fish being eaten by Japanese consumers, it didn't take long before traditional soy sauce consumption in Japan began to decline. To offset this change in diet, Kikkoman would have to rethink its marketing strategy at home and abroad. For one thing, it would have to move soy sauce from its traditional role as a condiment used primarily with Japanese and Oriental cuisine to a seasoning that could be used just as well with a wide range of Western cuisine.

Not only would Kikkoman have to step up efforts to market soy sauce as a viable condiment for a broad array of vegetables and meats, such as steak, lamb, pork, hamburger, and turkey, it would also have to come up with new soy sauce-based products such as glazes and marinades that Western palates would enjoy. While that may seem like a logical step to take, in the 1950s and 1960s, it represented a monumental shift in corporate philosophy.

While these ideas were being mulled over by Kikkoman's brass, Yuzaburo Mogi was in the United States earning an MBA from Columbia University. The years Mogi spent at Columbia between 1959 and 1961 would prove to be timely. Not only would he become the first Japanese to earn an MBA from Columbia, the 2 years spent in the United States would ultimately prepare Mogi to nudge Kikkoman into such unknown territory as the Big Foot Prairie.

Mogi's knowledge of the United States and its consumers would be critical—especially when it came time to convince Kikkoman's senior leaders, including his father,

Keizaburo, who was president from 1962 to 1974, that Kikkoman should open a manufacturing facility in the United States. The relationship between Keizaburo and Yuzaburo was a bit like that of a coach and a player. Keizaburo was a visionary who could see the need for international expansion, while Yuzaburo was given the task of carrying the ball toward that goal. The very act of sending Yuzaburo to Columbia was in essence a way of preparing for the "big game" on the North American continent. Then there were some key classmates Mogi met and got to know at Columbia who would prove critical to Kikkoman's success in setting up a plant in the United States.

But in 1961, when Mogi returned to Japan from the United States, he was still considered nothing more than a corporate pup who happened to be the scion of one of Kikkoman's founding families. Indeed, his first assignment after earning his MBA at Columbia was educational, if not humbling.

"I went to work in a soy sauce factory in Noda learning the business from the bottom up," recalled Mogi.

Mogi's time on the factory floor lasted about 6 months. It was just long enough to refamiliarize him with the nuts and bolts of Japan's oldest manufacturing industry following his heady experience in American academia. After that, he moved on to the accounting department where he exhibited flashes of the bold leadership that would eventually propel him to president and CEO, the position he holds today.

"In 1963 and 1964, I proposed installing a computer in the accounting department in order to replace the tedious clerical work," Mogi said. It was an audacious suggestion for a Japanese company in 1964. But the timing couldn't have been better. After all, in 1964, Japan was hosting the Olympic Games; it had built and unveiled its 135 mi/h *Shinkansen*, or "bullet train"—the fastest train in the world at the time; and it was blossoming into a true industrial power with heavy industries such as shipbuilding, steel, and automobiles replacing its postwar international reputation as a producer of cheap toys and Godzilla movies.

If Kikkoman was going to be part of this new industrial resurgence, it would have to modernize its operations, Mogi argued. It was an argument that resonated favorably with most of Kikkoman's senior leaders. So the same year that the Olympic torch was lit in Tokyo, Kikkoman installed an IBM 1440 mainframe computer to help handle its operating and management system—the first Japanese food company to do that.

But Mogi wasn't finished. In 1965, as a member of the corporate planning department, he began building a case for setting up a U.S. production facility. The story of how Kikkoman came to be the first Japanese company to set up a manufacturing facility in the United States is also a story of one man's persistence and resolve. It's a chapter in Kikkoman's history that didn't happen overnight, nor without some sweat, stress, and sacrifice. Mogi had begun building a case for a U.S. plant in 1965 when the corporate planning department was asked by top management to put together a cost study for the idea. In the mid-1960s, the planning department concluded that sales weren't high enough in the United States to warrant a plant.

But by September 1970, the picture had changed. Sales in the United States were up. As a member of the international operations department in 1970, Mogi organized a preliminary feasibility study that set out the rationale for a U.S. plant. Then, along with an exploratory team, he traveled to the United States to collect the data needed to support his plan. It was the beginning of a process the Japanese call *nemawashi,* a word that refers to the age-old practice of tending to the roots of rice plants so they will grow strong. Today, the term is used in corporate Japan to mean "consensus building." Following that preliminary trip, Mogi returned to New York in December and spent a month gathering more detailed information.

While in the United States, Mogi stayed with former Columbia University classmate Malcolm Pennington. Pennington, now a director of Kikkoman Foods, Inc., a U.S. subsidiary of Kikkoman Corporation, was a former IBM executive who was in the process of starting his own consulting company. Fate seemed to be pushing Mogi and Pennington back together 10 years after both had gone their separate ways following their graduation from Columbia.

It began when Pennington and his wife decided to travel to Japan to visit the Osaka Expo in 1970. During part of their 5-week stay, Pennington and his wife were invited to stay at a guesthouse on the Mogi estate in Noda. There, Mogi and Pennington spent long hours walking the estate grounds, talking about what it would take to set up a plant in the United States. After Pennington returned to his home in New York, he began putting together a marketing plan for his new company. Three days later, Mogi telexed and asked him to serve as Kikkoman's consultant in the United States.

"But the real beginning was when I met Yuzaburo at Columbia," recalled Pennington. "We had both joined the Toastmaster's Club. It was a gutsy thing for Yuzaburo to do because at that time his English was terrible. Toastmaster's is a great organization. Everybody makes a speech each week. Some members get speaking assignments a week before the meeting, but the rest aren't told the topic until just before they have to speak. Then they have 60 seconds to plan what they are going to say and 60 seconds to say it."

The topics thrown at Mogi ranged from the relations between Japan and Korea to answering such earth-shattering questions as: How would you describe the difference between Bridget Bardot and Sophia Loren?

Despite his struggle with English, Mogi plowed ahead. That kind of determination and perseverance made a lasting impression on Pennington. So did the fact that after 2 years of effort, Mogi spoke better English than most Americans.

Mogi lived frugally. Classmates say he carried his lunch in a brown bag and seemed to have only one suit.

"During his two years at Columbia, Yuzaburo lived in Room 1425 at John Jay Hall on 114th Street," recalled Pennington. "It was the least expensive place for a student to live."

In 1961, few of Mogi's classmates had ever heard of Kikkoman, which at the time was still called the Noda

Shoyu Co. For all they knew, Mogi could have been some Japanese war orphan who happened to find his way to New York. Nobody knew—or probably cared—that he was from one of the founding families of Japan's oldest continuously operated enterprise. After all, Japan in 1961 was not the economic powerhouse it is today. If anything, it continued to be regarded as an Asian backwater that was still trying to extract itself from the rubble of World War II.

"We really worried about him," Pennington said. "After graduation, the Toastmaster's Club had a picnic and Yuzaburo was asked what he was going to do. He said he had a job lined up. We were much relieved. Then he broke out a bottle of sake, and we warmed it over the fire and drank it."

Actually, Mogi had several job offers from American companies eager to recruit him. While the pay at the American companies was much better than the $100 a month he would earn in Japan, Mogi still decided to return to Kikkoman.

"I don't think any of these companies knew I was from one of the founding families of Kikkoman," Mogi said.

There is discernible emotion in Mogi's voice when he talks about his experiences at Columbia, despite the rigors of studying in a foreign language.

"I gained *konjo* at Columbia," Mogi said. Konjo is a term Japanese use to describe a sense of spirit or confidence.

"When I told my father I wanted to go to business school in the United States, he didn't agree," Mogi recalled. "This was 1958–1959 and the war hadn't been over that long. But my mother supported my decision."

Mogi had just graduated from Tokyo's Keio University, where he had read a Japanese translation of a book on management by Peter Drucker and had taken a course taught by an American professor named Whitehill from The University of North Carolina.

"I was really impressed by both," Mogi recalled. "This was very practical information. At the time, training in Japan was very theoretical. This was really the start of my business education."

There were several reasons why Mogi picked Columbia University over other American business schools. First, he says, Columbia is in New York, which is an international city, and many of Columbia's professors were international business consultants. Second, he liked Columbia's approach and philosophy of teaching.

"Some schools taught by using the case study method and some taught via lectures," Mogi said. "Columbia used a mix of both. It also had some great professors—men like William Newman, Charles Summer, and Joel Dean, who were well-known in the worlds of business management and economics."

Third, Mogi wanted to go to a university like Columbia that had a good mix of foreign students.

"I thought I could learn something from these foreign students," Mogi said. "And I did. I was totally internationalized."

In addition to a broad range of business theory, Mogi learned something that has proven to be almost as valuable—business English. It's a tool he insists has been critical when it comes to negotiating international business deals. But learning English wasn't easy, especially the way Mogi had to do it.

"I had to read at least 100 pages of textbook material every day and up to 1000 per week," Mogi said. "It was quite tough. But it taught me how to concentrate and how to handle hard work."

There was little time to play. His primary recreation each week was to sleep 9 hours on Sundays because Monday through Saturday he studied well into the night and barely managed to get 6 hours of sleep.

"My weight before going to Columbia was 68 kg (about 150 lb)," recalled Mogi. "By the time I graduated, I weighed just 58 kg (128 lb)."

While he may have lost weight at Columbia, he gained something else: insight.

"Basically, I learned that business principles were the same in the United States and Japan," Mogi said. "The differences occur in human relations. For example, Japanese executives will generally do everything they can before firing someone, but firing happens very quickly in the West."

But perhaps the most important thing Mogi learned at Columbia was how to understand America and Americans. As Mogi discovered during his campaign to open an American facility, that kind of knowledge was indispensable to Kikkoman's success in Walworth.

"I have maybe more understanding about American people than others at Kikkoman," Mogi said. "Sometimes, because of the cultural differences, Japanese cannot understand why Americans or Europeans behave a certain way, and Americans and Europeans can't understand why Japanese do things the way they do. If that kind of misunderstanding accumulates, hostile feelings can arise on both sides."

Understanding the differences between people leads to tolerance, and tolerance is critical when people of diverse cultures are supposed to work together. During the delicate negotiations to build the Walworth plant, Mogi's understanding of these differences would be crucial.

Not everything Mogi learned about North America was learned at Columbia, however. Nor was it learned by keeping his nose buried in books. During his stay in New York, Mogi never returned to Japan. But he did travel. Vacations and holidays were spent riding the rails of America. One such trip helped him gain a geographical understanding of the United States and Canada that would come in handy during the search for a U.S. factory site.

For a special low fare, he took a train from New York to Montreal, then to Toronto and over the Canadian Rockies to Vancouver, B.C. From Vancouver, he continued to Seattle, San Francisco, Los Angeles, the Grand Canyon, Kansas City, St. Louis, and back to New York. Along the way, he called on Japanese restaurants, which back in 1961 were few and far between.

"There were only eight in New York and there was only one in Montreal," Mogi said. "From Montreal to Vancouver, I couldn't find any Japanese restaurants. In Seattle, there were maybe 20 and in Portland, Oregon, there were 10. Most of them were using Kikkoman Soy Sauce." It was during his stay in the United States that Mogi learned some very practical lessons about promoting soy sauce as a product for Americans and other Westerners.

"As far as sales promotion is concerned, I learned the most effective way to sell our products was through demonstration," Mogi said. During his years at Columbia, he put that idea to the test more than once at trade shows, supermarkets, and food fairs. But Mogi learned something else, too. He learned that if Kikkoman was ever going to increase the size of the soy sauce market in America, it couldn't rely only on Oriental restaurants and stores that catered mainly to Asian clientele. It would have to create markets in the mainstream of American kitchens, restaurants, and supermarkets. It was knowledge that would stick with Mogi during the 1960s and into the early 1970s when he was hard at work trying to convince Kikkoman that a U.S. soy sauce plant would be a good investment.

In December 1970, during his second exploratory trip to the United States, Mogi, Pennington, and other members of the Kikkoman research team traveled all over America looking at potential sites and visiting machinery manufacturers and construction companies. But one state seemed to stick in Mogi's mind. Before leaving Japan, he had sent letters of inquiry to about 20 states requesting information on foreign investment.

"The first response was from Wisconsin," Mogi said. "I didn't know anything about Wisconsin at all, but I had a good impression about it because of its quick response to my letter."

During the exploratory trip, Mogi made a point of traveling to Wisconsin. It was just the first of many trips he would make over the next 2 years to the Badger State. By the end of December, Mogi and his team had returned to Japan armed with what they considered to be the kind of documentation needed to make a strong case for a U.S. plant. At the top of the list was the fact that sales of soy sauce in the United States were increasing. In addition to increasing sales, there were other compelling business and financial reasons to build the plant, Mogi said.

Mogi argued that there were three advantages to having a plant in the United States over an older strategy that had begun in 1967. That scheme called for the shipping of bulk soy sauce to San Francisco in giant tanks where it was bottled by the Leslie Food Company, a subsidiary of Leslie Salt Company based in Oakland.

"The first advantage was that we could save freight costs," Mogi said. "Soy sauce is a very heavy product to ship. But the product itself isn't that expensive. That means that freight costs compared with sales are quite high. So eliminating freight costs from Japan to the United States was an attractive element.

"The second advantage was that we could save duty," Mogi continued. "At that time, U.S. duty on soy sauce was 6 percent.

"The third advantage was that the raw materials needed to make soy sauce were already in the United States," Mogi said. "We were buying wheat and soybeans in the United States and shipping them to Japan. If we built a factory in the United States, we wouldn't have to pay ocean freight for raw materials. Furthermore, the distance between the raw materials and our factory would be shorter, which meant we would need less inventory—another big savings."

While these were strong arguments in favor of a U.S. plant, Mogi also knew there were some downsides.

"There were actually two demerits to a U.S. plant," Mogi said. "Although we would save on ocean freight, inland freight would be more because when we shipped products from Japan we off-loaded them at regional ports like Seattle or New York. But after we built a factory, we would have to ship the product from the factory all over the United States, which means an increase in inland freight costs."

Another downside, Mogi said, was the amount of investment required for a U.S. facility.

"Machinery, especially, would cost a lot more in the United States," Mogi said. "Readymade machinery in the United States isn't so expensive, but special-order and custom-built machinery is. Most of the machinery used in making soy sauce is specially made. That means some would have to be shipped from Japan, which meant another outlay for ocean freight and duty."

Mogi knew that the cost of building a plant in the United States in 1972 would be high, especially at a time when it took 360 yen to buy $1. In fact, says Mogi, the amount of the proposed investment of more than $10 million was about two thirds of the total paid in capital of Kikkoman in 1972.

"Today, that wouldn't be considered big money, but back then it was," Mogi said.

The sizable investment notwithstanding, Mogi prepared a report containing all the pluses and minuses and handed it to the head of the international operations department.

"I gave my proposal to my boss, Mr. Hiroshi Ishikawa, who was a board member," recalled Mogi. "At that time, there were two board meetings each month. He presented it at a board meeting in February 1971. There was no decision. Later, at another board meeting in early March 1971, he presented the proposal again and once again there was no decision."

Mogi was not deterred. In fact, he expected it. Kikkoman, after all, was an old, conservative company steeped in tradition. The idea of making shoyu—a 100 percent Japanese product—in America was daring, and it required an entirely new mindset.

"There were some in the company that viewed Yuzaburo Mogi's idea of building a plant in the United States the same way they viewed the World War II battleship *Yamato* or the Great Wall of China—glorious failures," recalled Kaichiro Someya, director of the office of the president and former general manager of the foreign operations department.

The *Yamato*, the largest battleship ever built, was the pride of imperial Japan until the 63,000-ton vessel was sunk off Okinawa by American planes in 1945, thereby rendering the technology of seagoing leviathans obsolete. The celebrated Great Wall of China was equally unsuccessful in keeping barbarians out of the Middle Kingdom.

A factory in the United States would be just about as effective, many of Kikkoman's leaders argued. For one thing, the proposed plant would have the capacity to turn out 9000 kL (about 2.4 million gal) of soy sauce its first year. But because of market size, the actual production was less. Kikkoman's sales in the U.S. market in 1971 amounted to about 6000 kL (about 1.6 million gal).

"Senior leaders at the time didn't believe a U.S. plant would be successful," Someya said, sitting in Kikkoman's Tokyo offices. "Yuzaburo Mogi had a tough time selling the idea. A lot of people criticized him, even though he was the eldest son of one of the founding families. He was considered radical, even crazy, to propose such an idea.

"Proposing an American plant was a high-risk project for Mogi," Someya continued. "He didn't have to take this kind of a risk. Most were convinced that it was his destiny to become president of the company. So why take such a risk? If the project failed, he would be discredited and it would end his chances of becoming president. But he took the risk anyway.

"Why?" Someya asked, a wry smile on this face. "Because Yuzaburo Mogi is a risktaker."

But as Someya is quick to point out, Mogi is a risktaker who understands and calculates the odds.

"Yuzaburo's risk on this issue was supported by the profound knowledge contained in an international mind," Someya said. "Yuzaburo Mogi was a very independent man inside a very conservative company."

Finally, on the third try in late March 1971, Mogi's proposal was accepted by the board. As in most Japanese companies, Kikkoman's board of directors didn't take a formal vote, recalls Mogi. There was some pro and con discussion as members weighed the proposal.

"There was neither strong opposition nor strong support for the idea," Saheji Mogi, one of the directors, told Yuzaburo Mogi. "Everybody was silent. Then your father made the decision to go ahead."

Now that the idea of a U.S. plant had been approved, Mogi was faced with a new set of problems. First, Kikkoman's team had to select a site in the United States; then it had to get zoning approval for it from the community and its residents. Mogi wasted no time. The selection process began less than a month later in April 1971.

"We compared the West Coast, the Midwest, and the East Coast," Mogi recalled. "We didn't think the East Coast would be an appropriate place, mainly because our sales in the United States were larger in the West than the East. We decided that both the West Coast and the Midwest were very competitive."

Eventually, Mogi and Pennington both agreed that the Midwest made more sense for Kikkoman's first U.S. plant than the West Coast. A big reason was because the Midwest had all the raw materials needed to make soy sauce.

"Once we decided on the Midwest, we had to decide where in the Midwest," Mogi recalled. It was decided that no matter where the plant was built, it needed to be within 100 mi of at least one major market.

"We screened 60 candidates in Michigan, Indiana, Illinois, and Wisconsin. Most were in Illinois and Wisconsin. We eventually dropped Michigan and Indiana because of freight costs. Then we reduced the number to six, and all six happened to be in Wisconsin."

Mogi returned to Japan with his six candidates and in August 1971 returned to Wisconsin with a final decision team that included his father, Keizaburo. The team scoured the six sites, examining them from the air in a helicopter provided by Wisconsin Power & Light and on the ground by car.

"Then, in September, we voted," Mogi said. "Everyone agreed that the site in the township of Walworth was the best."

One reason the 200-acre Walworth site was chosen, recalls Pennington, is because the property has five sides to it—a configuration considered auspicious by Shinto priests, who were consulted later in Japan. After discussions with engineers in Japan, Mogi, Pennington, and Ishikawa retained the Elkhorn law firm of Godfrey, Neshek, and

Worth to buy options on the land. The firm had been recommended by another law firm in Washington, D.C.

"Mogi and Pennington had been talking to the county officials about rezoning," said Milton Neshek, a partner in the firm who is also general counsel and a director of Kikkoman Foods, Inc. "They knew that it was zoned A-1, which meant that it was the highest quality farmland. But the county had told them it was willing to rezone the property to industrial. What they didn't know, however, was that under Wisconsin law, the three-man town board in Walworth had the power to veto any rezoning that the county did."

Instantly, there was a big obstacle in Kikkoman's road to Walworth, recalls Neshek. It was as if a gnat had suddenly turned into a sumo wrestler—a sumo wrestler that couldn't or wouldn't be moved.

"It became apparent right away that there was opposition at the town level, and this great controversy suddenly exploded right in our faces," Neshek said.

The town was split over the issue. On one side were those who feared that Kikkoman would turn Walworth into a mini-Chicago replete with smokestacks, soot, and strange odors. Others were angered that prime farmland would be gobbled up to build a factory, something considered close to a mortal sin in a part of the country that boasted some of the best topsoil in the nation.

Then there were those who still harbored ill feelings toward the Japanese because of World War II. Latent racial feelings were also evident, especially among those who saw the Japanese as little more than World War II Hollywood caricatures or who worried out loud that Japanese soy sauce brewers would run off with every available Wisconsin milkmaid.

On the other side were those who were convinced that a plant like the one Kikkoman was proposing represented less of an environmental threat than an economic opportunity.

With battle lines drawn, Kikkoman suddenly found itself preparing for what some have called "The Battle of Big Foot Prairie."

7 CHAPTER

A Soy Sauce Plant Grows in the Land of Cheese

November 9, 1971, was a relatively mild autumn day in southern Wisconsin. A few stubborn leaves still clung to the trees, and the skies over Walworth were filled with honking geese and ducks flying south in tight V formations. No need for heavy coats. No need for gloves or caps with earflaps. Nevertheless, winter was on the way. You could smell it. It was in the air. It would only be a matter of a few short weeks and the area's recently harvested corn and soybean fields would be a vast sea of chalky snow stretching from horizon to horizon. Only an occasional herd of Holstein or Guernsey dairy cattle would break the monotony of white pastures covered with snow.

But the weather was the furthest thing from the minds of executives and lawyers representing the Kikkoman Corporation. It had only been about a month since Kikkoman had decided that a 193-acre parcel of land that once made up the old Harold Wright and Gordon Weter dairy farms just north of Walworth's city limits was the place it wanted to erect the biggest soy sauce plant ever constructed outside of Japan.

It had been a 6-year process that Yuzaburo Mogi had shepherded from beginning to end. Today, as Kikkoman's president and CEO, Mogi can look back and chuckle about those days. But he wasn't laughing on November 9, 1971. Far from it. As a member of Kikkoman's international operations department, Mogi had put his reputation and career on the line. And now, with the perfect site selected, there was a good chance that the people of Walworth might decide they didn't want Kikkoman and its soy sauce factory. In fact, it was that very point that would be the sole topic of discussion during one of the liveliest town meetings in Walworth's history.

It's little wonder that Yuzaburo Mogi was a very nervous man. For years, he had nudged, politicked, and used all the powers of persuasion he could muster to convince Kikkoman's senior leadership that a soy sauce factory in the United States made sense. It had been a tough sell. After all, in 1971, Americans knew as much about soy sauce as they did about sumo wrestling or sashimi. They might be able to tell you that it came from Japan, but beyond that, it would be a blackout.

What possible reason could there be for building a soy sauce plant in a place like Walworth? Some of Kikkoman's brass wondered. Despite the fact that Kikkoman's soy sauce market in the United States was increasing incrementally, it was still minimal (about 6,000 kL, or 1.6 million gal in 1971), recalls Malcolm Pennington, Yuzaburo Mogi's old Columbia schoolmate and Kikkoman's primary business consultant in the United States. And here was a plant that had the capacity to produce 9000 kL, or some 2.4 million gal, during its first year of operation. In addition, few Americans could tell the difference between the top-quality brewed shoyu made for centuries by Kikkoman and the inferior chemically produced soy sauce that abounded in many of the nation's 17,000 Chinese restaurants unless they compared the two in a side-by-side taste test.

But people with vision aren't readily put off by such arguments. And Yuzaburo Mogi was among the most visionary executives at Kikkoman in 1971. Not only had he spent long hours building his case, but he had spent considerable political capital trying to transform his vision of a Kikkoman plant in the United States into reality. And now, on November 9, 1971, Mogi was fully aware that he had passed the point of no return.

If the people of Walworth rejected the plant, it would be an enormous setback to Kikkoman's plans, and possibly to Mogi's career. This was a fact that Tom Godfrey wouldn't really come to appreciate until much later. Godfrey, an attorney from nearby Elkhorn, had been hired by Mogi just 2 months earlier to represent Kikkoman's interests in Wisconsin. Before his death in July 1996, Godfrey talked about the fateful night of November 9, 1971, and the events leading up to it.

"I remember Yuzaburo called from Washington, D.C., to ask for a meeting on Saturday, September 8," recalled Godfrey, a big, jovial, bespectacled man with a full head of snow white hair. "But I had to attend a football game and I put Mogi off until Monday. I will never forget that as long as I live because I thought I came that close to losing the account. We had been recommended to Mogi by a law firm in Washington."

On September 10, Mogi walked into the offices of Godfrey, Neshek, and Worth and announced that he wanted the firm to represent Kikkoman in its plans to build a soy sauce factory in Walworth.

"I remember thinking 'Whaa? A soy sauce plant?'" said Godfrey. "I couldn't believe there was any kind of a soy sauce market in the United States to warrant such an investment. I don't think I had ever tasted any soy sauce in my life and I know I hadn't heard of Kikkoman. That shows you how much I knew."

Godfrey and partner Milton Neshek sat down with Mogi and began discussions that would evolve into a relationship that still exists. Not only would both Godfrey and Neshek become members of the board of Kikkoman's U.S. subsidiary, Kikkoman Foods, Inc., along with former Columbia schoolmate Malcolm Pennington; they would also become Kikkoman's right arm in the United States.

"Yuzaburo wanted us to negotiate the final details of the purchase of two pieces of land adjacent to one another on the northwest edge of Walworth," Godfrey said. "We asked about zoning, because this was prime agricultural land they were looking at.

"And Mogi said: 'Oh, we have been assured by everyone that will not be a problem. Period.'

"Well, guess what?" Godfrey continued. "All hell broke loose. Not because it was a Japanese company, not because it was a soy sauce factory, not because of anything else, but because for a farming community to take 200 acres out of production is a sin in this part of the country."

Godfrey and Neshek quickly mounted a full-bore crusade on behalf of Kikkoman. The first step was to deal with the three-member town board, Godfrey recalled.

"Politics in Walworth in those days was pretty unsophisticated," Godfrey said. "Two of the town board members didn't even know that they had the same vote as the chairman. They assumed the chairman had full authority to do everything. It turned out the town board was divided with one member opposing the plant, one supporting it, and another undecided."

When Godfrey discovered that there was resistance to rezoning on the town board, he called Mogi who jumped on a plane and flew in from Tokyo. He was in Walworth the next day, racked with jet lag and just in time for a crucial meeting with the three-member town board.

"I remember getting an emergency call from Tom Godfrey, our lawyer in Wisconsin," Mogi said. "He said there had been some opposition to us. I remember the meeting was held in the home of the board secretary. There were many questions, and I answered many of them myself."

With Mogi at the meeting were Godfrey, Neshek, Malcolm Pennington, and one of Mogi's assistants from Kikkoman. Mogi, who at the time was only 36 years old, explained to the town board just what soy sauce is, how it is made, and how Walworth would benefit from having a plant in the area.

"I was very nervous," Mogi recalled. "If the town board refused to approve us, I was afraid it would give us a very bad image. If we had to go to another town, I was afraid that they might say no to us, too. At the beginning, I thought the town board might be against us because we are a Japanese company or because we were making a product that wasn't well known by Americans.

"But during the meeting, I could see it had nothing to do with the company's nationality or even the product we made," Mogi continued. "The opposition was because of the rezoning request. They didn't want to lose prime agricultural land to a factory."

After the meeting, it became apparent to Godfrey and Neshek that a lot of *nemawashi* was needed in Walworth before people would feel comfortable about having a plant in the area that made a product most had never heard of or used.

"When we left that meeting, I was really very disappointed," recalled Godfrey. "The town board didn't really seem to care whether the factory came or not. It just couldn't see the benefits of having a company like Kikkoman in Walworth. I felt that this was a great opportunity, not only for the town of Walworth, but for the whole area."

Indeed, the Walworth facility uses some 15,000 acres of soybeans that are grown in southern Wisconsin and northern Illinois. Another 15,000 acres of red spring wheat comes from western Minnesota and North Dakota. Then, there are residual benefits for local suppliers and other businesses.

"We went to work and began organizing a campaign geared to winning over as much support for Kikkoman and its project as possible," said Godfrey. "But about halfway through it, I realized that the question of odor was very important to a lot of people around town. I called Yuzaburo in Tokyo and suggested that I come to Japan and check out the Noda plant to see if there were any unpleasant smells."

Mogi told Godfrey to come ahead. There was nothing to hide. When Godfrey got to Japan, he drove up to Noda and spent a good half day sniffing around Kikkoman's various facilities.

"Nothing smelled unpleasant," said Godfrey. "Boy, was I relieved."

When Godfrey returned to Walworth, he and Neshek shifted their campaign into high gear. One of the first ideas was to get the word out about Kikkoman, soy sauce, and Japan—not necessarily in that order. The 30th anniversary of the Japanese attack on Pearl Harbor was about to be observed in the United States, and there was still some residual anti-Japanese feeling among those who had lost sons and husbands in the war. Nearby Janesville, a town about 30 mi away, was home to a regiment that suffered 90 percent casualties during the bloody 1945 battle for Iwo Jima, and a halfhearted campaign was mounted to block Kikkoman's plans. That fizzled when the local newspaper reported that the veteran spearheading the opposition had never seen combat during World War II, nor, in fact, had ever left the United States.

As it turned out, there was less reason to be worried about old wartime animosities than about the perceptions the people of Walworth had about a plant that would turn out millions of gallons of a product few had ever seen or used.

Then there was the sheer novelty of it all. This would be the first wholly owned Japanese manufacturing facility ever built in the United States. It would not be a spin-off or a joint venture or a strategic alliance.

And there was something else, too. The first Japanese manufacturing facility in the United States would be turning out a 100 percent Japanese product. It wouldn't be selling American technology back to America in the form of cars, television sets, or VCRs. Shoyu was about as Japanese as you could get.

"While there may have been some remnants of bad feeling from World War II hidden in the background, I think the biggest fear was of the unknown," said Neshek. "No one had ever heard of soy sauce. They didn't know what it was.

"I remember talking one day to Milt Pflaum, one of the three members of the town board, out at his farm," Neshek recalled. "He was the one member of the board who was still undecided about the plant. We put our feet up on a bale of hay and he asked me about soy sauce. I tried to explain to him that it was a condiment, an all-purpose seasoning, a natural product made with no environmental impact.

"He looked up at me and said: 'You know, I also heard that it's good for baldness if you rub it on your head.'"

Neshek had to think about that one for a moment.

"I told him I'd never heard that," Neshek said. "Then I said: `But if you try it and it works, let me know.'"

That encounter would be only one of several dozen Neshek and Godfrey would have over the next few weeks with local residents at Grange meetings, Farm Bureau groups, churches, ladies clubs, and Rotaries. Their plan of attack was the same in each case. They would explain that the production of soy sauce was a clean and natural process that needed clean air, clean water, top-quality soybeans, wheat, and rock salt. It was a natural production process that was nonpolluting and environmentally friendly.

"Looking back on it, it was probably a good thing that we had some opposition," said Neshek. "It forced us to go to the community to sell the idea of a Kikkoman plant. We had to explain what we were doing and why we were doing it. That gave the town the opportunity to get to know Kikkoman and it gave Kikkoman a chance to get to know the town."

Neshek and Godfrey continued their rounds of local Grange halls and farm organizations. Sometimes they even talked to farmers in their homes.

"We ate a lot of Jell-O," recalled Neshek, referring to one of the staples of midwestern farm meals. "You know, when a typical farm family serves something to eat like sandwiches, you always have Jell-O with whipped cream."

Neshek and Godfrey got prominent farmers to organize meetings with other farmers, and they brought Yuzaburo Mogi in to talk with them.

"We wanted them to see that these were real people who needed the products they grew to make their products," Neshek recalled. "We really had to sell them on the idea that Kikkoman was a company that would be a tremendous asset to this community...that it would promote economic development, jobs, and would be a good corporate citizen."

After weeks of making the rounds to talk to farmers, local businesspeople, and other residents, Neshek and Godfrey were still not sure how people felt about the Kikkoman proposal. And they still weren't sure which way the town board would go on the issue. That was important because the county zoning board had already approved the rezoning of the 200-acre parcel from agricultural to industrial use. However, Wisconsin law gave the town board of Walworth final veto power, and it had 30 days to approve or disapprove the county's rezoning action. Its chairman, Milton Voss, was opposed to the Kikkoman plant, recalls Neshek. Another member, Milt Pflaum was still straddling the fence, and a third member, John F. Altpeter, was for it.

"I can remember getting word that some Japanese company wanted to come in and build a plant," recalled Altpeter, the only surviving member of the old town board. "I remember Yuzaburo Mogi coming to Walworth to talk to us. He talked better English than I do."

After listening to Mogi, Altpeter was convinced that the Kikkoman plant would be good for Walworth.

"For one thing, the plant would be using local grain grown by local farmers," recalled Altpeter. "That would be good for us. Then, a lot of local people would be hired by Kikkoman. Young farmers could work at the plant and still run their farms. That, too, would be good for us.

"I felt that even though a soy sauce plant would be built on farmland, it would still be a form of agriculture," Altpeter said. "First, Kikkoman would be buying wheat and soybeans from farmers, and Kikkoman had said it would rent out portions of the land it wasn't using to farmers. Also, a lot of people working at the plant would be farmers."

Nevertheless, still troubling to many was the idea of removing 200 acres of farmland from agricultural production to build a factory. *The Times,* a local weekly newspaper, decided to investigate. It ran a story on an interview with a local agricultural expert who said that the 200 acres Kikkoman was buying was not the prime agricultural property everybody thought it was.

"The expert said that after a few inches of good topsoil, the land was mostly gravel," recalled Fred Noer, then editor of *The Times*. "That doesn't make for good crops."

That revelation was significant, but the town board was still unable to make up its mind. With the town board still undecided on the issue, Neshek took a calculated risk and asked then Democratic Governor Patrick Lucey to come down to Walworth and enter the fray at the local level. It was a risk because Walworth County was and is a fiercely Republican enclave that hadn't elected a Democrat to any office in more than 100 years. Asking a Democratic governor to intercede on Kikkoman's behalf could prove to be counterproductive.

Governor Lucey had been involved in the process from the beginning. He knew how important and prestigious it would be for Wisconsin to land the first Japanese manufacturing facility ever built in the United States. It would be a major coup for Wisconsin. While Kikkoman was still in the site-searching mode, Governor Lucey had provided a Wisconsin Power & Light helicopter to fly then Kikkoman President Keizaburo Mogi, Yuzaburo Mogi, and other members of the search team to several sites, including three in the Madison area. Then Lucey had hosted a reception for the group on the roof of the state capitol building. The group had then choppered down to nearby Lake Geneva to look at three other sites, including Walworth.

With that kind of support at the state level and with the subsequent decision by the county zoning board to rezone the property, everything seemed fine in September. But that was certainly not the case in November. It was at this point that the town board decided that the best way to handle the issue would be to have a town meeting and let the people of Walworth decide. In essence, the town board was looking for a way out of making a decision, recalls former town board member Altpeter.

"I think town board chairman Milton Voss wanted to let the people decide for themselves so the town board wouldn't have to make the decision," said Altpeter. "It was such a hot issue at the time."

The idea of a town meeting was one way to deal with the question, but no matter what happened at the meeting, it wouldn't be legally binding. The town board would still have to make the decision, even if it was by default. If the town board didn't veto the county zoning board's decision to rezone the property from agricultural to industrial within 30 days, the rezoning would become law, recalled Neshek. Still, a town meeting would allow the town board to get a good reading of local sentiment about the Kikkoman plant, and it could use that as a bellwether in deciding which way to go.

"All the cards seemed to be falling into that one meeting," recalled Neshek. "We knew we had to pull out all the stops."

And that's exactly what Godfrey and Neshek did. Some state politicians such as state Senator James Swann, a Republican, were in favor. So was Republican Assemblyman Clarence Wilger. But this wasn't a matter of partisan politics. Governor Lucey, a Democrat, was a vociferous supporter, whereas Elnora Wickstrom, a prominent local Democrat, was dead set against the plant. Wickstrom had organized a lot of opposition to the Kikkoman proposal, Neshek recalled.

"A few days before the town meeting, I called Governor Lucey hoping to get his assistance in moderating Wickstrom's views," Neshek said. "Lucey asked me if he should come down to Walworth for the meeting on November 9—a place that in modern history had never elected a Democrat to anything.

"I had to make a split-second decision," Neshek said. "Would Lucey's presence in a Republican stronghold like Walworth hurt our cause? I went kind of numb for a moment. Then I said, 'Governor Lucey, we'd be honored to have you come.' As it turned out, it was the best thing that we could have done."

Lucey, now retired and living in a Milwaukee suburb, thought long and hard about what he should say at the meeting. "I remember on the way down trying to think of what I should and shouldn't say," he said. "It was pretty obvious that I shouldn't say that these are the people who brought you Pearl Harbor."

One question that kept going around and around in Lucey's head was: Why Walworth County?

"Of those counties on the border with Illinois, like Kenosha, Rock, and Racine, it's by far the most conservative," Lucey recalled. "I mean there are a lot of families there that go back to pre-Civil War days. This was a solid Republican stronghold with Republicans going back at least four generations—maybe more. In the 1930s and 1940s, it was a hotbed of isolationism…not the kind of place that may welcome a foreign company, especially one from a country we had been at war with just 30 years before."

When Lucey walked into the tiny weatherboard town hall—a building that could seat 75, but which was packed with almost twice that many people—jaws dropped, recalled Godfrey.

"Here was a Democratic governor walking into this rock-ribbed Republican town…well, it was an incredible sight and people did double takes," Godfrey said. "Then he gave one of the best speeches anybody could give on behalf of Kikkoman. You could have heard a pin drop."

Neshek, who was also there that night, remembers that you could almost cut the electricity that was in the air. Some of it may have been his own. After all, he had purposely neglected to tell Republican Senator James Swann that Lucey was coming, and he didn't know what kind of explosion the governor's entrance might set off.

"People were hanging from the rafters listening to speaker after speaker talk for and against the plant," Neshek said. "Most were for it. Then Lucey spoke."

Lucey told the 140 or so people crammed shoulder to shoulder in the town hall that Walworth couldn't afford to pass up such an incredible opportunity to have an old and prestigious company like Kikkoman become part of their community. He told the crowd how the state of Wisconsin had checked out Kikkoman's financial stability, its background, and had decided it was a top-flight company.

"The state has been working months to attract this 300-year-old agribusiness company to our area," Lucey said. "In building a new plant to make its famed soy sauce in Wisconsin, Kikkoman will provide 100 new jobs, add about $8 million to the local tax base, and generate about $200,000 in real estate taxes each year for the town of Walworth. That will provide substantial tax relief for the other citizens of Walworth and Walworth County.

"Look, I'm a Democrat and I know most of you are Republicans. But I don't care about that. Kikkoman's presence will be a major advance in the rural and economic development of our state," Lucey said. "Both Walworth County and Wisconsin stand to gain tremendously from this decision. This thing shouldn't be turned down."

After Lucey finished talking, Swann—one of Lucey's fiercest political rivals—kept the crowd captivated when he got up and urged the town of Walworth to heed what Lucey had just said.

"We don't want to give this company a chance to go elsewhere," Swann said.

The next day, *The Times* carried a rare picture of Lucey and Swann on its front page. It showed the two men shaking hands and under the picture was the caption: "Finally, They Agree on Something!" The paper also carried a rather significant story about that historic meeting in Walworth's modest town hall. The story pointed out that during the meeting an informal vote on the issue was taken. Only those who were residents of Walworth township were allowed to vote.

"Governor Lucey and I were holding our breath as that vote was taken, I'll tell you," recalled Neshek.

The vote, which was not binding, showed 54 in favor of allowing the county's rezoning to stand, with 14 opposed.

After the vote, Neshek and Governor Lucey slipped out of the meeting and drove to the Abbey Hotel on nearby Lake Geneva to discuss another issue over a few drinks. At the time, Lucey was in the process of restructuring Wisconsin's higher education system. That called for combining the state's two boards of regents—one which served the state's smaller universities and one which served the University of Wisconsin in Madison. It was a redundant system that could be made more efficient and less costly with the elimination of one of the boards. Neshek, who had been appointed to the state board of regents by Lucey's Republican predecessor, supported Lucey's proposal while the state's Republicans were opposed to it.

"We were mainly rejoicing about the vote in Walworth over the rezoning proposal," said Neshek. "Governor Lucey and I both thought the victory was won. But as it turned out, it wasn't that easy."

A few days later, with only about 10 days left for the Walworth town board to veto the county zoning board's decision to rezone the property from agricultural to industrial, Neshek got a call from Fred Noer, the editor of *The Times*.

"You need to know what's happening," Noer told Neshek. "The opposition is circulating petitions saying that the vote at the town meeting only consisted of a small percentage of voters and that Kikkoman's proposed factory could still be defeated.

Neshek and Godfrey went back into action.

"We rolled up our sleeves and got everyone in our law firm out collecting petitions in favor of Kikkoman and the plant," recalled Neshek. "We overwhelmed the opposition. In the end, it was more than two to one in favor. That was their last gasp."

Nevertheless, both Godfrey and Neshek were still in a state of high anxiety until the very last day of the 30-day deadline when the phone rang in their office.

"It was the clerk of the town board," said Godfrey. "He said, 'Come on down. We want to talk to you.'"

Godfrey and Neshek looked at one another and shrugged. What now? they wondered.

"We went down to the town hall and the three board members were sitting there waiting," recalled Godfrey.

"'You know,' Voss said, 'we have decided to do nothing. That way, nobody is going to pin us down as to whether we are right or wrong on this issue. If we don't vote, we haven't taken a stand.'"

Nevertheless, no vote was the same as a vote in favor, and the next day the 30-day deadline for a town board veto came and passed without any action.

"We had won—finally," recalled Godfrey.

On the day after the 30-day deadline passed, Godfrey and Neshek had a picture taken. It showed both of them holding the new county zoning permit that would allow Kikkoman to build its plant. Underneath the picture, they wrote the following facetious caption: "You were right. There was no problem."

In fact, recalled Godfrey, the 6 weeks he and Neshek had worked on the rezoning issue were the hardest 6 weeks they had ever worked. It hadn't been any easier for Yuzaburo Mogi, according to Kaichiro Someya, director of the office of the president and former general manager of the foreign operations department.

"Yuzaburo made more than 30 trips to the United States between the fall of 1970 and January 1974," Someya said. "He was so exhausted and weak that he came down with pneumonia and had to spend several months in the hospital afterwards."

It had been a period of incredible stress for Mogi and his father, Keizaburo, who, as president of Kikkoman, had put a lot of faith in his son's drive to build a U.S. plant. Now, there was one final hurdle. They would have to build the plant and get it operating as quickly and efficiently as possible.

During the site-selection process, Kikkoman had hired the Austin Co., a Cleveland-based international design, engineering, and construction firm, to build the new facility. Austin, Kikkoman learned, was one of the very few American design and construction companies that had the expertise to build a Japanese soy sauce factory.

Unlike the mild weather that prevailed the day of the crucial Walworth town meeting, on the day ground was broken for the new Kikkoman plant, the earth was frozen as solid as the gray stonewalls of Tokyo's Imperial Palace. It was January 18, 1972, barely a month after construction crews had cleared some 50 acres that would be the site of the first buildings and just about 2 months since Kikkoman and its small squad of Wisconsin supporters had successfully battled to get the site rezoned. The temperature was about 20° below zero, recalled Godfrey.

"We were very worried about the people from Japan—especially the ladies—who weren't used to this kind of weather," he said.

To make sure those involved in the actual groundbreaking could get their shovels into the frozen tundra, gas-jet heaters had been brought in 2 days earlier to keep the ground thawed.

Despite the subzero temperatures, the groundbreaking went off well. Mercifully short speeches were made, and afterwards the whole contingent moved to the Abbey Hotel on nearby Lake Geneva for cocktails. It was at this point in the day's events that Godfrey recalls a rather significant encounter with Kikkoman President Keizaburo Mogi. "Keizaburo took a liking to me," Godfrey said. "During the cocktail party, he walked up to me and poked his finger playfully in my chest and said in broken English: 'You are Kikkoman now; you must take care of us!'"

It was a timely admonition and one that Godfrey took very seriously. A few days later, with the Kikkoman brass back in Tokyo, Godfrey drove down to the construction site to see how things were going.

"The foreman was getting ready to pour the footings for the building in temperatures that were still 20° below zero," recalled Godfrey. "I called a few of the construction people I knew around the area and asked them about that. They told me it would be disastrous because the concrete wouldn't set up properly. It would freeze and honeycomb."

Godfrey returned to the construction site and cornered the site manager.

"You're not going to pour concrete today," Godfrey said.

"Oh yeah, who says?" the site manager replied.

"I do. I represent Kikkoman and what I say goes on this project!"

"Well, we'll see about that!" the manager said. Within minutes, he was on the phone to his bosses in Cleveland.

Godfrey, standing nearby, watched the belligerence fade from the face of the site manager as his bosses in Cleveland explained the way things would work.

"If that guy there in Walworth says 'no,' then we aren't going to pour any footings," they told him.

It was the last confrontation Godfrey would have with those putting up Kikkoman's factory.

"I felt good about it because I was doing what Keizaburo Mogi had asked me to do," Godfrey recalled. "I was taking care of Kikkoman."

A year later, the plant was up and operating—just in time for the global oil crisis of 1973 which sent much of the world economy into a tailspin. Kikkoman was not immune. Higher oil costs translated into higher energy costs for the new factory. That resulted in more headaches and stress for Yuzaburo Mogi, who was still Kikkoman's point man for the Walworth plant. Back in Tokyo, there were still many who considered the Walworth facility a mistake. Some had even privately predicted its failure. The events of 1973 made them seem like prophets.

"I was worried, but I was still confident," recalled Mogi. "My feeling was that within 5 years the operation would be all right."

Tobias J. Steivang, president of the Walworth State Bank, recalls that many in Walworth were still worried about something else in 1973, even after the assurances given at the town hall meeting.

"Some people were still concerned about the smell and noise that a soy sauce plant would make," said Steivang, who was born and reared in Walworth. "As it turned out, the factory was and is a nonevent. It's not noisy. The odor from brewing is not objectionable. We've got farms around here that put out worse odors than the smell of roasting wheat.

"The Kikkoman plant is now a part of the landscape around here," Steivang continued. "The company has really worked hard to be a part of this community."

In early June 1973, 17 months after the frigid groundbreaking, Kikkoman's first soy sauce plant in the United States turned out its first bottle of soy sauce. And on June 16, 1973, in much more temperate weather than the groundbreaking, Kikkoman held its official grand opening. As far as Walworth was concerned, it was the mother of all grand openings.

"It was an event the likes of which had never been seen before in this area," Godfrey remembered. "We had 1200 people. It was a big blowout. Kikkoman insisted that everything be first class. So it was. Everything was *ichiban* (number one). There were Japanese dancers and taiko drummers. It was really spectacular."

One of those on hand that day was high school student Dave Rasmussen. Rasmussen and other members of the Walworth High School band were called on to play "Kimigayo," the rather slow and solemn Japanese national anthem.

"I'd never heard it before and it took a lot of practice to get it right," recalled Rasmussen, who went on to law school, opened a practice in Walworth, and became the Walworth village president. "We must have gotten it right, because I never heard any complaints."

Less spectacular than the grand opening were Kikkoman's numbers, which for 1973 and 1974 were very bright red.

"We had a very bad year that first year," Mogi recalled. "The second year was also bad. Both were worse than I expected. I remember during that time people in the office back in Tokyo would look at me and ask, 'Oh, are you all right?' It was as if they were trying to say to me, 'You spent a lot of money in Walworth and the plant is losing money, so how do you feel?'"

Like everybody involved in the Walworth operation, Mogi wasn't thrilled.

"Still, my confidence didn't disappear," Mogi said. "Of course, I was a little bit afraid. But I was still young...about

38 then...and young people have enough energy to handle that kind of stress."

By 1975, the Walworth plant had become profitable on a calendar-year basis, and by 1977, the company had offset all the losses incurred during the previous years, Mogi says. Since those early days, sales have increased an average of 10 percent per year in the United States and production at the plant has grown 12 times to about 21 million gal. It helped, recalls Pennington, that those who had set up the Walworth plant under a subsidiary called Kikkoman Foods, Inc. (KFI), had used very conservative numbers.

"Our initial costs were far below those in the original Japanese plan," said Pennington. "Labor costs, for example, turned out to be 30 percent lower than what Tokyo had expected. And this was long before the yen made its big rise against dollar."

The kind of thinking that went into those numbers was largely the result of Yuzaburo Mogi's insistence that the new U.S. factory be operated as an American plant and not as a Japanese plant, recalled Godfrey.

"I remember our organizational meetings were held in makeshift quarters," Godfrey said. "That's where we created our operations manual. That was a really interesting experience, I can tell you. It taught us a lot, but most of all, it taught us patience. You know how Americans are. We want to get things done...get moving...go, go, go. That's our style, you know: 'On Wisconsin' and all that."

But the Japanese were a much more cautious lot, recalls Godfrey. It was like sitting in a room full of samurai planning a big battle. Everything had to be examined down to the minutest detail.

"I remember we would take a paragraph of the operations manual and present it to the Japanese side," Godfrey said. "We would discuss it awhile in English. Then the Japanese would lapse into Japanese and talk about it for maybe an hour. Meanwhile, the Americans in the room would talk about baseball or basketball or something else. Finally, the Japanese would return with the paragraph and say 'Okay, next please.'"

Even though Mogi had promised that the Walworth operation would be an American operation, he told Godfrey, Neshek, and Pennington that at least initially the key managers in the plant, as well as its foremen and biochemists, would be Japanese. The reason was nothing more than experience. There were most likely no Americans who had ever made naturally fermented soy sauce, and even if there were, you could be sure that none had made it the way Kikkoman did.

"It took us probably 2 months to get the organizational manual written," Godfrey said. "Meanwhile, Yuzaburo was running back and forth between Walworth and Tokyo. He participated in all of our meetings, all the way through."

After the manual was created, the next step was to hire staff for the Walworth plant. This was a critical milestone in the plant's initial success.

"Each employee we hired was handpicked," Godfrey said. "We met as a group: Yuzaburo Mogi, Milton Neshek, Malcolm Pennington, and myself. And we each interviewed every employee who was hired. There were originally 20."

The very first was a Japanese-American woman from Chicago named Mamie Asari, whom Kikkoman discovered quite by accident. Asari was recommended to Kikkoman by the local Pontiac dealer who was leasing cars to Kikkoman executives. For years, Asari and her husband had driven up from Chicago to buy new cars from the dealer, and when he heard Kikkoman was looking for an American who could speak Japanese, he suggested Mamie.

Pennington drove to Chicago, took Asari to lunch, told her about Kikkoman's plans in Walworth, and offered her a job. Asari, who was working part time for a Chicago real estate developer, was reluctant to leave Chicago and turned down Pennington's offer. However, a subsequent meeting with Yuzaburo Mogi changed her mind.

"He said Kikkoman really needed my help. The first bunch of Japanese who came to Walworth had small children, couldn't speak English, and were really scared...I felt sorry for them," recalled Asari, who spent her first year or so commuting from Chicago. Each week, she would buy several hundred dollars worth of Japanese food and deliver it to each of the Japanese homes.

In the early 1970s, the gap between Japanese and American culture was much greater than it is today, said Asari, who proved to be a critical bridge between Nippon and the Big Foot Prairie. She helped organize activities for the Japanese wives, helped them get driver's licenses, shop, and deal with local schools.

"Back in the 1970s, a lot of Japanese families were afraid to go into town because of the language and cultural barriers, but today the people assigned from Japan study English before they come so it's not as difficult for them," she said.

Despite the job offer she received, Asari still went through the most detailed job interview she has ever experienced.

"Kikkoman is very thorough," recalled Asari. "You'd have thought I was going into the civil service."

Only one employee wasn't hired using this formula, and that proved to be the only one that didn't work out.

"We hired an American personnel manager on the basis of a recommendation without interviewing him," recalled Godfrey. "He turned out to be the wrong person for the job."

While the management team looked for a new personnel manager, Godfrey served in that role for almost 6 months. Finally, Kikkoman hired William Nelson to be personnel manager. Godfrey, Pennington, and Neshek had contacted him through an executive recruiting firm.

"Godfrey did the first interview and approved him," recalled Pennington. "But we all talked to him before he was hired."

Nelson, now a member of KFI's executive committee and vice president of administration, was given some good advice by Godfrey when he was hired:

"I told Bill, 'Now, this is not going to be a bed of roses...I'm throwing you into a real interesting situation because you will have to deal with diverse nationalities,'" Godfrey said. "He understood and he has done a beautiful job."

Godfrey's warning to Nelson was not simply idle chatter. Making a traditional Japanese product in Wisconsin with American workers—many of whom had never seen or used soy sauce—would not be easy. And it wasn't. It was only a matter of time before the clash of cultures, attitudes, and work habits would supplant the honeymoon that stretched from the groundbreaking to the grand opening.

"We ran into problems with the fact that the parent company felt that Japanese executives could totally manage the operation," said Godfrey. "At the time, only the personnel department had an American manager."

Today, only seven Japanese employees work at the plant, and Americans have been fully trained in the Kikkoman system of soy sauce production. But that wasn't the case when the U.S. plant opened. Kikkoman sent 14 Japanese managers and supervisors to Walworth, along with their families.

"Purchasing was to be handled by a Japanese fellow, the warehouse foreman was Japanese, and other key positions were all Japanese," recalled Godfrey. "As it turned out, some of these people were disasters. They didn't understand Americans or the American way of doing business."

As might be expected when employees from two different cultures were thrown together, there were a few hitches and hiccups as the plant got untracked in its early stages. But it wasn't long before these were ironed out. Meanwhile, Mogi was being true to his philosophy that calls for the localizing of all foreign operations as much as possible.

"This is not such a new idea for us," said Mogi. "We have been doing business in Noda for more than 300 years where the idea of coexistence and coprosperity has been important to our success. It was only natural for us to apply the same concept to our first U.S. operation."

And that's what Kikkoman did. Mogi ordered the new factory to find as many suppliers as possible among local American companies—a lesson that Japan's auto industry took a lot longer to learn. Among the early success stories was a small Wheatland, Wisconsin, metal fabricating company called Ultra-Fab, which built a double-walled stainless steel mixer to Kikkoman's specifications and remains a supplier today. Others include Chicago Plastics, which makes plastic spouts for Kikkoman's 1-gal cans; McCormick Stange, which is a spice supplier; Cargill Corp., which supplies wheat; and Archer Daniels Midland, which supplies soybeans.

"We recruited as many local people as possible for most jobs and then we promoted them as they learned," Mogi said. "Modern soy sauce factories are capital intensive, so we don't have to recruit a large number of people."

But there is another point when it comes to hiring Americans for some of the top positions in the plant.

"There is no school or institution in America that teaches the technology of soy sauce production, and that's a reason why we couldn't hire an American production manager in 1973," said Mogi, who is quick to point out that the plant does have a number of American production managers today, mainly because Kikkoman itself has provided the kind of long-term training that it takes to hold down the position. Today, Americans head the plant's personnel, accounting, and brewing departments, as well as the bottling and warehouse operations.

Another important element is Kikkoman's philosophy of requiring Japanese employees and their families to live separately from other Kikkoman-employed families in the many small communities that surround the Walworth facility.

"Sometimes this wasn't easy for Japanese, especially the families of our employees," said Mogi. "Few wives and children spoke English. But gradually, they learned to speak English and they became accustomed to the lifestyle in Wisconsin. They joined the local PTA, the Rotary Clubs, and so forth. They became part of the community."

That kind of activity goes all the way to the top. In 1987, Mogi was named honorary ambassador to Japan for Wisconsin by Governor Tommy Thompson, a position he takes very seriously. He is also a former member of the Business Development Council for the state of Wisconsin.

Typically, Japanese employees and their families spend about 5 years on an assignment in Walworth before they are rotated back to the parent company in Tokyo.

"We have tried to delegate authority to local management in Walworth as much as possible," said Mogi. "We don't manage by remote control from Japan. If we have an idea or an opinion in Japan, we come to Wisconsin to discuss it with local management."

It's that kind of autonomy that has allowed Kikkoman Foods, Inc., in Walworth to grow into one of the most productive of all of Kikkoman's worldwide plants, according to Neshek. Beyond the autonomy afforded Walworth is the way the parent company in Tokyo views those who are assigned to Wisconsin, he adds.

"Japanese executives come over to Wisconsin for 5-year stints and usually return to more prominent positions in Japan," Neshek said. "The U.S. subsidiary is considered a place to learn and to get on the fast track at Kikkoman."

Unlike many American companies that all too often don't seem to know what to do with returning managers, those who return to Tokyo from Walworth and the company's other plants in Singapore and Taiwan are viewed as valuable repositories of knowledge that can be leveraged and used.

"We have learned that in order to do business successfully in America, it is necessary to follow the American way of management," Mogi said. "I know there are a lot of people in America who have a great interest in the system of Japanese management, and some suggest that the Japanese system should be adopted in the United States.

"However, adapting the Japanese system of management in the United States is not easy and is, in fact, often dangerous because too often Americans overlook the disadvantages of the Japanese system," Mogi added.

For example, one characteristic of the Japanese system is the bottom-up decision-making process. An advantage to this system is that implementation is usually very quick because, in the process of moving an idea from the bottom up, many people can participate in the decision making. This means that, once the decision is made, everybody involved is ready to implement it quickly with no residual resistance.

"However, a disadvantage to this bottom-up system is that it takes much, much longer to reach a decision because it requires a consensus from all those people who were involved in examining the idea," Mogi said. "Too many Americans look at the quick implementation time, but overlook the longer amount of time it takes to make a decision."

There is one area of Japanese management that seems to have gained a lot of converts in Walworth. That's the heavier emphasis the Japanese in general, and Kikkoman in particular, tend to place on the human side of management. Not only is that reflected in the productivity of the Walworth plant, it can also be seen in the kind of employee loyalty Kikkoman has earned. The average worker at the Walworth plant has been with the company more than 10 years and earned about $24 an hour in salary and benefits in 1996. The company's reputation as a fair employer that genuinely cares about its workers has resulted in a deep stack of employment applications—about 750 in 1997.

Richard Kottke, production manager for the critical steps of pressing and filtration of soy sauce, calls Kikkoman's Walworth management style a "trust-based" system with an emphasis on patience and long-term thinking. "There's not a time clock anywhere in the plant," said Kottke, who grew up on a farm in nearby Sharon, Wisconsin. "Employees just sign in when they come in and sign out when they leave. Nobody abuses it because people like the idea that the company trusts them."

Kottke calls Kikkoman's management style a combination of Japanese and American systems.

"What I like about Kikkoman is the focus on problem solving rather than assigning blame," said Kottke, who joined the company in 1973. "Too many American managers look to blame somebody for a problem. Here, the objective is to find the problem, fix it, and prevent it from happening again—not to blame somebody. This is a company that respects people."

Outside the walls of Kikkoman's sprawling plant, there are similar sentiments about the company.

"There's no doubt that Kikkoman has had the biggest single impact on this area from an economic standpoint than any other company, ever," said Walworth village president, Dave Rasmussen. "They had a big impact on salary scales. When it opened up, Kikkoman was paying the kind of wage that you had to drive to Chicago to get."

But that's not all.

"As far as giving to the community, Kikkoman is the undisputed leader," Rasmussen said. "They are such good corporate citizens. They have set the standard for everybody else."

In 1993, in honor of its 20th anniversary in Walworth, the company set up the $3-million Kikkoman Foods Foundation. It has since contributed some $200,000 for cultural, educational, and economic development in Walworth and other Wisconsin communities. But long before the foundation was established, Kikkoman executives and employees were donating time and money to everything from the Future Farmers of America and 4-H organizations to thousands of dollars to local school districts in appreciation of the extra time and effort they took to educate the children of Japanese employees.

"I wish I could clone Kikkoman throughout the state," said Katherine Lyall, president of the University of Wisconsin system and head administrator for all higher educational institutes in the state university colleges. "It puts its money where its rhetoric is. It contributes thousands of dollars in unrestricted funds to the University of Wisconsin Foundation as well as to all 15 college campuses in the system.

"The time and money Kikkoman has given to the University of Wisconsin system have made a margin of difference between our doing something ordinary and doing something excellent. That's what being a good corporate citizen is all about."

8 CHAPTER

A Culture of Selective Risk:

The Enduring Secret of Kikkoman's Success

Somewhere in Denver, Colorado, are the remains of what is most likely the first Japanese-built and managed soy sauce plant in the continental United States. Unfortunately, just where the plant was located and what happened to it remain a mystery.

But one thing is fairly certain: Some 25 years before the forerunner of today's Kikkoman Corporation was formed and 80 years before Kikkoman built its plant in Walworth, Wisconsin, a member of Japan's shoyu-producing Mogi clan came to the United States with the idea of setting up a soy sauce plant.

The year was 1892 and Shinzaburo Mogi—barely 20—had a bold idea. He would go to the United States and produce Japanese shoyu. After all, hundreds of thousands of Chinese and Japanese had immigrated to the United States in the late nineteenth century, and more were sure to come seeking a better life. As representatives of Asia's so-called chopstick cultures, these people would need a supply of top-quality soy sauce.

Given the resourceful and entrepreneurial history of the Mogi clan, Shinzaburo's actions aren't surprising. After all, Kikkoman's founding matriarch, Shige Maki, had escaped from Osaka Castle and the troops of Shogun Ieyasu Tokugawa in 1615 and had made her way to Noda where she and her son were among the early soy sauce makers in Japan.

Then there was Saheiji Mogi, whose Kikkoman trademark was first accepted by the Tokugawa shogun family in 1838. By 1868, the Mogi clan was shipping soy sauce to Hawaii and California—traveling with some of the first Japanese immigrants to both places. In the 1870s, the Mogi family entered its soy sauce in several world's fairs in the Netherlands and Austria, and in 1879, the Kikkoman brand name was registered in California.

The Noda Shoyu Brewers' Association (an organization dominated by Kikkoman's founding Mogi and Takanashi families and a forerunner to today's Kikkoman Corporation) had even planned to set up an agent in New York in 1885 to handle soy sauce imports to the United States.

And in a move that foreshadowed Yuzaburo Mogi's days at America's Columbia University, Saheiji Mogi, VII, sent his first son to England's Cambridge University between 1884–1886, according to a company chronicle printed in Japanese.

Another member of one of Kikkoman's founding families, Hyozaemon Takanashi, XXIX, also attended Cambridge in 1927, returned to Japan, and joined the Noda Shoyu Co. in 1930. Takanashi, who died in 1988, became a member of the board in 1942, was named managing director in 1947, and became president of Kikkoman International, Inc. (KII)—Kikkoman's first U.S. unit—in 1957.

There was nothing timid about the Mogi and Takanashi clans—not when it came to promoting and selling their shoyu. In fact, the main Mogi household and its five branches, along with the Takanashi family (cofounders of today's company), have a long history of selective risk-taking that still permeates the company and influences its current CEO, Yuzaburo Mogi.

So going to the United States, while a gutsy move in 1892, was not out of character for a member of the Mogi family. In fact, it seemed like a good idea. Here was opportunity. Here was a young country of incredible bounty that offered a young man like Shinzaburo Mogi room to grow and prosper, even if he never produced a single bottle of soy sauce. Indeed, even the Chinese characters used by the Japanese to write "America" are translated as *Beikoku,* or "rice country"—an acknowledgment of America's reputation as a land of vast agricultural abundance.

But Shinzaburo Mogi's entrepreneurial spirit may not have been the only driving force in his decision to come to the United States. An unwritten rule within today's Kikkoman Corporation and its forerunner allows just one male member from each of the eight family branches to join the company each generation. It's a system that creates a vigorous, but healthy, competition for power between family branches. Each branch selects a candidate (usually the first son) and invests heavily in his education in the hopes that he will ascend to the top. Those not selected have to seek their fame and fortune elsewhere.

"Only one child can join the company from each branch each generation," explained Kikkoman President and CEO Yuzaburo Mogi, who comes from the Homare branch of the Mogi family. "But there is no guarantee that each person who joins from each branch will become president or a board member. There is a kind of healthy competition between the families for power in the company."

It's a system that seems to have worked. No one branch has had more than two presidents since the company was formed in 1917, said Mogi. A look at Kikkoman's corporate genealogy reveals that the Kashiwa branch, Yuzaburo Mogi's Homare branch, and the Mogi Sa branch have each had two of the company's ten presidents since 1917. The mainstream Honke household has had one president.

Under unwritten rules, every family group in the clan can select a son to work for the company. In some rare cases, other sons have been allowed to work for the company, but with the understanding that they will probably never be on a path to the top.

In other cases, a member of a clan that already has a member in the company from the current generation can be adopted by a family that has no representative. That's what happened in the case of Yuzaburo Mogi's younger brother, Kenzaburo.

Kenzaburo, or Ken as he prefers, was born in 1938 in Noda City. Like Yuzaburo, he was a member of the Homare branch of the Mogi clan. Because he was not the first son, Ken joined the Bank of Tokyo after graduating from Tokyo's Hitotsubashi University.

"I had no intention of quitting the bank and entering Kikkoman," he said sitting in Kikkoman's Tokyo offices where he is managing director. "But even if I did, the unwritten law about allowing only one person per generation from each branch to enter the company would have kept me out. It's a wise rule. It allows us to maintain a certain balance and harmony among the founder families."

Ken Mogi may not have had any plans to join Kikkoman, but others had different ideas when they used the "adoption" procedure. Adoptions are common practices among the Mogi families and are usually done to keep the family name alive. A year after he had joined the Bank of Tokyo, the head of the Honke household, which is the original Mogi family, asked to meet with Ken's father.

"I would like your son to become the successor of the Honke household," he said.

"My father and I were both surprised at this, and for 5 or 6 months afterwards, I continued to refuse," Ken said. "I didn't want to leave the Bank of Tokyo. I liked the banking business. I had a degree in economics. I spoke English and I liked international banking. Back in the early 1960s, when all this happened, the Bank of Tokyo was Japan's most international bank."

During the 6 months that Ken continued to spurn the offer to join Kikkoman by becoming the Honke household's chosen successor, he was under almost constant pressure to change his mind.

"Not only my parents but also uncles and aunts came to me and said that I'd better become the Honke successor and enter Kikkoman," Ken said.

Ken Mogi finally gave in to the pressure after 2 years with the bank and in 1962 joined Kikkoman as a representative of the Honke household. His career at Kikkoman has taken him from the factory floor in Noda through the accounting department, the international operations department, the corporate planning department, the corporate development department, and the board room. Along the way, he was sent to Harvard University where he earned an MBA.

It was an entirely different story for Shinzaburo Mogi, however. As the fifth son of the Kashiwa branch of the Mogi family, he did not join the family business in Japan. Shinzaburo's oldest brother, Shichiroemon Mogi, became the first president of the Noda Shoyu Co., the company that would eventually evolve into today's Kikkoman Corp.

But even though he never joined the family business, one can't help feeling that Shinzaburo Mogi was fortunate. In 1892, Japan was in the apogee of its Meiji era (1868–1912). It was a time of unprecedented enlightenment for Japan. The country had been effectively "closed" to the rest of the world since 1603 when the first of the Tokugawa shoguns decided to keep out such "corrupting" influences of Western civilization as religion, technology, and progressive political systems. For 265 years, that's exactly what each succeeding generation of Tokugawa shoguns did. While the Tokugawa period resulted in one of the longest periods of domestic peace and political harmony in Japanese history, it also stifled technological innovation, social development, and political maturation.

Now, with the nineteenth century drawing to a close, Japanese were venturing out of Japan to Europe, the United States, and other parts of Asia in an effort to learn everything they could about the rest of the world. It was a time of incredible discovery for Japan, and young Japanese men and women like Shinzaburo Mogi were like human sponges, absorbing all they could from everywhere they journeyed.

Not much is known about Shinzaburo Mogi's early years in the United States, but it's not for want of trying. Kenzaburo Mogi (not to be confused with Yuzaburo Mogi's younger brother Kenzaburo), who is Shinzaburo's great grandnephew and currently a director in charge of Kikkoman's domestic marketing division in Japan, traveled to Denver in the early 1980s in search of information about his great-granduncle and his attempt to make shoyu in America.

Kenzaburo, the son of Katsumi Mogi, who served as Kikkoman's president from 1980 to 1985, had heard the stories of this little-known member of the Mogi clan for years—some of them from Keizaburo Mogi, who served as president of Kikkoman from 1962 to 1974, when he became chairman of the board.

"Though Kikkoman started brewing soy sauce successfully in Walworth, Wisconsin, in 1973, we have to remember that we are not the first [from the Mogi family] to try to make shoyu in the U.S.A.," Keizaburo Mogi, who died in 1993 at the age of 94, often pointed out in an obvious reference to Shinzaburo Mogi.

Despite Kikkoman corporate lore that told of Shinzaburo's efforts in the United States, when Kenzaburo Mogi arrived in Denver, he found that time had eroded both memories and physical evidence of his great-granduncle's venture. But he was nevertheless able to learn that Shinzaburo Mogi had indeed managed a soy sauce plant in Denver in 1907. Unfortunately, the operation was not successful, Kenzaburo learned after a meeting with a man who apparently worked with Shinzaburo Mogi at the plant. It may have been due to its location in the Mile High City—far from the settlements of natural Japanese and Chinese customers in California. Or it may have been the lack of marketing ability or perhaps the U.S. market simply wasn't ready for soy sauce in the early twentieth century.

But failure in Denver didn't stop Shinzaburo Mogi from pursuing his dream of making soy sauce in North America. After Denver, he apparently helped manage a soy sauce plant in Toronto, Canada. Eventually, he settled in Chicago where he was involved in the trading business—

including the importing of Japanese (most likely Kikkoman) shoyu to the United States.

But the idea of making naturally brewed shoyu in the United States still intrigued Mogi, and in the 1920s, he discovered that a small plant in Columbia City, Indiana, was turning out Japanese style soy sauce under the name Oriental Shoyu Co., Inc. The company had been founded by a Japanese man named Shinzo Ohki. One of eight children, he was born in 1884 into the family of a shoemaker in Kamakura, Japan. As a boy, Ohki was apprenticed to his uncle's rice wine warehouse. He saved his money and in 1901, barely 17, he immigrated to the United States. Ohki eventually made his way to the Midwest and settled in Columbia City. There he entered high school, graduated, and eventually went on to New York, where he graduated from New York University.

After New York, Ohki settled in Detroit where he set himself up in business as a tea merchant. He also began importing soy sauce in bulk form from Japan, bottled it, and sold it with his tea. It didn't take long for Ohki to discover that there was a tremendous demand for soy sauce among the area's Asian community.

Ohki returned to Columbia City, Indiana, recruited a partner, incorporated as the Oriental Shoyu Company, Inc., and set up a soy sauce bottling business in an old canning plant. With demand for soy sauce growing, Ohki reasoned he could be more successful if he learned how to make soy sauce himself. So in 1917, he returned to Japan, learned how to make soy sauce, obtained a formula for naturally brewed shoyu (along with a wife), and returned to Columbia City where he began making soy sauce on his own.

Ohki got some help from the U.S. Department of Agriculture in producing the necessary microorganism needed to produce a "koji culture," which is required for naturally fermented soy sauce. Within a few years, his soy sauce was available in most stores specializing in foods, condiments, and products for America's growing Asian community.

It was in such a store that Shinzaburo Mogi, who was now working for the Yamato Trading Co. in Chicago, found Oriental Shoyu Soy Sauce during the 1920s. Intrigued—and perhaps still fascinated by the idea of producing naturally brewed Japanese shoyu in America—Mogi traveled to Columbia City to see the operation for himself. He found that the Oriental Shoyu Co. used a production and natural fermentation process that took about 24 months. Impressed with Ohki's operation, Mogi invested in the plant and became a major stockholder in the company until the outbreak of World War II when his property (as was the case with all Japanese immigrants) was seized by the U.S. government under the Alien Property Custodian Act.

Mogi had returned to Japan shortly before the beginning of World War II and died in 1946. Before his death, he showed his daughter, Katsuko, the stock certificates he still held for the Oriental Shoyu Co.

"They're worthless now," he said, and tore them up.

In fact, the Oriental Shoyu Co. continued to produce soy sauce until 1961, when it was sold to Beatrice Foods, Inc. and became a part of La Choy Food Products Co. The operation was eventually moved out of Columbia City, and the company's natural soy sauce making process was discarded for the faster and less labor intensive chemical method. Today, the only evidence of the Oriental Shoyu Co. is a few crumbling remnants of the factory's foundation in Columbia City.

At its peak, the Oriental Shoyu Co. turned out about 30,000 gal of soy sauce a year—a far cry from the 18 million gal produced annually by Kikkoman's Walworth, Wisconsin, plant. And even though Kenzaburo Mogi's research found that his great-uncle wasn't directly involved in the creation of the Oriental Shoyu Co., there is a certain satisfaction in knowing that a member of one of Kikkoman's founding families was a major investor and contributor to what is perhaps the first successful Japanese shoyu operation on America's mainland.

Shinzaburo's efforts in the United States were never sanctioned by Noda Shoyu Co., Kikkoman's corporate predecessor. And Shinzaburo never joined the company that his brother became the first president of. Nevertheless, Shinzaburo Mogi was an innovator who had an innate understanding of the kind of selective risktaking that still drives people like Yuzaburo Mogi today. And while his ventures in the United States were totally independent of Kikkoman, they are still worth remembering because they may, in some small way, have influenced a visionary leader like Keizaburo Mogi to be unwavering in his support for the U.S. plant that today's CEO, Yuzaburo Mogi, eventually convinced Kikkoman to build.

The problem for Shinzaburo Mogi, of course, was that he was a bit ahead of his time. It would be decades before mainstream America would become enamored of things like sushi, sashimi, sukiyaki, yakitori, and Japanese teppanyaki cooking—all foods that depend on soy sauce for flavor enhancement. Even Chinese food during that era was only marginally popular, and fewer people still were familiar with an Asian condiment called soy sauce.

"Naturally brewed soy sauce is, after all, a very Japanese product," said Kaichiro Someya, director of Kikkoman's office of the president and former general manager of the foreign operations department.

The original meaning of the Japanese word for seasoning (*chomiryo*), explains Someya, refers to the period of time when fruit ripens, thereby improving its flavor. Interestingly, the Japanese character for the word *results* is read as "ripe fruit." It's no accident that the words *seasoning* and *results* are so closely intertwined in the Japanese language. Nor is it coincidental that soy sauce and Japanese food are so closely related. Indeed, soy sauce is such a common part of Japanese cooking that some culinary experts say it's the one thing that distinguishes Japanese cuisine from all others.

"It's doubtful that there is anyone [in Japan] who eats sashimi with ketchup, mayonnaise, or Tabasco sauce," Someya wrote in a company marketing strategy document. "But even if some adventurous people were to do so, would they feel that they were really eating Japanese food? It's safe to say that soy sauce is at the origin of the flavor of Japanese cuisine."

"In the past, Americans didn't seem interested in Japanese food or culture," Someya wrote. "In fact, at the time, Americans living in the United States didn't seem to like any Oriental foods and flavors."

In the marketing strategy report, Someya summed up the differences between traditional soy sauce-dependent Japanese cuisine and Western cuisine:

"Traditionally, Japanese culture values simplicity. Regarding the basic necessities of life—food, shelter, and clothing—the fundamental Japanese way of thinking is to make the most of the basic materials."

That isn't the case with most Western foods, however.

"For example, the main area of competition among French chefs is the sauces," Someya said. "The food itself plays a supporting role and the sauce has the main role."

Then there is the relative simplicity of most Asian dishes when contrasted with the heavy sauces and gravies that often envelop Western food.

"Plain white rice alone is enough to whet a Japanese person's appetite," said Someya. "The main factors that determine its deliciousness are the quality of the rice, the amount of water put in, and the temperature at which it is cooked.

"The number of Westerners who understand the deliciousness of simple white rice is few. It is doubtful that anyone born and raised in Japan would do this, but there are Westerners who pour soy sauce over rice. That could indeed be considered a fortunate thing for the maker of soy sauce if Japanese consumers did this."

You don't have to dig very deep into the American experience to discover something else about the America that Shinzaburo Mogi found himself living in during the early part of the twentieth century. Here was a country of predominantly white Europeans that was mostly ignorant of Asian cultures, cuisine, and condiments. Its people often demonstrated an incredible disdain and ignorance of anybody or anything from Asia.

"Some Americans even called soy sauce 'bug juice,'" recalled a Kikkoman official. "And certainly, no one at the time would ever have thought that soy sauce could grow into a worldwide business the way it has today."

According to the Soyfoods Center in Lafayette, California, throughout most of the twentieth century—possibly until the early 1960s—most Americans viewed soy sauce as a Chinese product used to season Americanized Chinese foods like chop suey and chow mein. Most soy sauce sold in the United States was sold in stores catering to Oriental customers and was marketed under Chinese names such as La Choy, Koon Chun, Pearl River, and Chun King.

More important, most of this soy sauce was chemically produced. That means it is made by combining hydrolyzed vegetable protein (HVP) with salt water, corn syrup, and artificial coloring. The result is a soy sauce that is an opaque, dark brown color with a distinctly salty taste. Unlike the naturally brewed soy sauce made by Kikkoman, which takes several months to produce via a complex fermentation process and which contains an intricate array of flavors, chemically produced HVP soy sauce takes just a few hours to produce.

During Shinzaburo Mogi's early years in the United States, he was probably aware that naturally fermented soy sauce was being made in Hawaii and that there may even have been a few futile attempts to make it on the U.S. mainland. But in the early part of the twentieth century, almost all soy sauce used in the United States was still being imported, and much of that was coming from China. Having grown up in Noda as a member of Japan's leading shoyu producing family, Shinzaburo must have been raring to show American consumers what "real" top-quality shoyu was supposed to look and taste like.

Unfortunately, the America of the early twentieth century hadn't "discovered" the Pacific Rim yet. Most of the nations of the region were still little more than colonial enclaves. There was no Malaysia, no Singapore, no Indonesia, no Vietnam, no Laos, no Cambodia. Instead, there were vast expanses of land and people that were still under the rule of Great Britain, France, and the Netherlands. Those countries not under control of the European Raj were no better off. Many were still backward places with very little experience in the emerging political philosophies of the day. In fact, Taiwan itself was under control of the Japanese (1895–1945), and Korea came under Japanese rule between 1910 and 1945.

China itself was a land in political turmoil, its provinces ruled by warlords who would later become part of a broader struggle between the Chinese Nationalists of Chiang Kai-Shek and the Communists under Mao Tse-Tung (Mao Zedong). And Japan, at least in the minds of most Americans, was an Asian backwater that had only decided to open its doors to the rest of the world barely 30 years before. It was a nation still cloaked in a mantle of inscrutability. Only a handful of Americans knew anything about the culture, and fewer still had any competence with the language.

Indeed, the America that Shinzaburo Mogi entered was a nation with strong European biases. Oriental food, ideas, and culture were simply not a meaningful part of the U.S. experience the way they are today. Soy sauce was virtually unknown in the kitchens and restaurants of America, unless they happened to be Japanese or Chinese kitchens. In fact, it was not until the mid-1950s and 1960s that soy sauce began to enter the mainstream of American cuisine, and even then, it was a trickle, not a torrent.

But as small as it was, even that trickle can be largely attributed to an astute move that Kikkoman made in 1957. That was the year that Kikkoman set up its first marketing arm in the United States—San Francisco-based Kikkoman International, Inc. The company's first U.S. subsidiary was given the task of overseeing North American sales.

It did its job well. By 1983, Kikkoman had captured more than 40 percent of the U.S. retail soy sauce market and became the number one seller. In 1994, its share was about 50 percent of the 40-million-gal retail soy sauce market, while La Choy—Kikkoman's biggest U.S. competitor—owns about 30 percent of the market. Japan's Yamasa and San-J have also entered the U.S. soy sauce market, making it more competitive than it has ever been. In 1997,

Kikkoman's share of the U.S. retail soy sauce market had increased to 51 percent.

Interestingly, Kikkoman's U.S. efforts have resulted in a pleasant and spontaneous response in Japan. Japanese consumers, aware of Kikkoman's success in marketing soy sauce in the United States as a "universal" seasoning that can be used to bring out the flavor of a broad range of Western foods and dishes, have also begun to use it on Western-style dishes that they prepare at home or order in restaurants. Shoyu is no longer seen only as a traditional Japanese seasoning that you dip your sashimi or sushi in or use with other types of indigenous Japanese cuisine. Instead, it has become almost as universal at home as it has in the United States.

It was a process that Kenzaburo Mogi witnessed firsthand during the 6 years he spent in San Francisco between 1980 and 1986. Four of those years he spent with JFC International, a subsidiary that is the largest importer of Oriental foods in the United States. For another 2 years, he was assigned to Kikkoman Marketing and Planning, Inc., a research and development arm of Kikkoman Corporation that was recently moved to Chicago where it has been charged with creating new products for the U.S. market.

Like his great-granduncle before him, Kenzaburo Mogi would be faced with the challenge of introducing a little-known Japanese product to the mainstream U.S. market. The product? Kikkoman brand tofu. Tofu is a protein-rich, low-fat, low-calorie food made from solidified soya milk. The resulting soft and smooth bean curd can be cut up in squares and used as a meat substitute in salads, stir-fry dishes, and soups.

Sales were good when Kikkoman brand tofu was introduced in 1985, recalls Kenzaburo Mogi, but the rise of the yen against the dollar made it difficult to import the product to the United States and still make a profit. Nevertheless, like soy sauce, tofu found a home with mainstream American consumers, especially those who are health conscious. While not nearly as prolific as soy sauce,

Kikkoman brand tofu can be found today on supermarket shelves from New York to Los Angeles.

When Kenzaburo Mogi returned to Japan, he joined Kikkoman's foreign operations department and quickly became involved in what he says is probably Kikkoman's first joint venture in a foreign country. While not nearly as risky as setting up a full-blown soy sauce plant on the plains of Wisconsin, Kikkoman's venture in Taiwan was still another example of selective risktaking.

The process began in 1987 when a Japanese pharmaceutical company with a small food division informed Kikkoman that a Taiwanese company it did business with was interested in getting technical assistance in improving its naturally brewed soy sauce plant in Taiwan. Kenzaburo Mogi wrote to the company (President Enterprises) and discovered that it had set up a soy sauce plant in 1976, but their results had not been very successful.

He also learned that President was looking primarily for Japanese technology and little else. However, Kikkoman wasn't only interested in providing technical help. It wanted to go much further and create a joint venture that would allow it to produce soy sauce in Taiwan.

"In November 1987, I went to Taiwan to meet the top management of President Enterprises and to take a look at its plant," recalled Mogi. "The plant wasn't bad."

At the time, naturally brewed soy sauce was only about 35 percent of the market in Taiwan. Today, it is almost 45 percent and is growing. In 1997, Kikkoman's share of Taiwan's 86,000-kL annual soy sauce market was about 7 percent. Mogi and others at Kikkoman decided that with its technology and some upgrades to President's equipment, it could produce Kikkoman-quality naturally brewed soy sauce in the plant for the Taiwan market. But the Kikkoman brain trust was thinking further ahead than that. In 1988, Kikkoman exported some 300 kL of soy sauce to Taiwan, but it was subject to heavy duties.

First, the Kikkoman brass reasoned, it would make much more sense to make soy sauce in Taiwan with a Taiwanese partner than to continue shipping it from Japan.

Second, given the contentious political climate between Beijing and Taipei, Kikkoman knew it could not use the plant in Taiwan as a platform for export to China. But having a joint venture with a Taiwanese company to produce naturally brewed soy sauce might provide Kikkoman with valuable knowledge about the much larger mainland Chinese market.

"Our joint venture with President in Taiwan may help ease the way into China," said Kikkoman President and CEO Yuzaburo Mogi. "These seeds that we are planting now [in Taiwan] can grow into something much bigger in the twenty-first century."

Yoshiyuki Nogi, general manager of Kikkoman's overseas trade department, says the seeding process is already well under way for what is the world's largest soy sauce market.

"Soy sauce consumption in mainland China is about 4.5 million kL (about 1.1 billion gal) per year," he said. "By comparison, the Japanese market is 1.2 million kL (about 320 million gal)."

While the company already exports some soy sauce to China from a plant it opened in Singapore in 1983, given the enormous size of the Chinese market, it is only a token amount. The Singapore plant exports to more than 44 countries in Asia, Europe, and Oceania, according to Dr. Masatoshi Noguchi, managing director of the Singapore plant.

"We expect increased sales in Asia…even though our soy sauce is priced one and one half to two times higher than most local soy sauces," said Noguchi, who adds that consumers throughout Asia have more discretionary income than ever before and are spending it on higher quality products, including Kikkoman Soy Sauce.

While that pattern may not be quite as pronounced in mainland China, there are nevertheless Chinese consumers who can afford and who want the higher quality, naturally fermented soy sauce that Kikkoman produces. Although that may seem to some a bit like selling ice to Eskimos or taking coals to Newcastle, it really isn't.

Despite the fact that the predecessors of modern soy sauce originated in China around 300 B.C., according to the Soyfoods Institute of Lafayette, California, demand still outstrips production in China. (Those precursors were a sauce made from meat or fish called *jiang* and another seasoning called *chi* made from soft, salty fermented soybeans.)

"There are maybe 4000 soy sauce manufacturers in China, but they can't meet demand," said Nogi. "So we are not viewed as a threat."

Then there is the soy sauce itself. Japanese-style shoyu, which Kikkoman excels at making, is much different from 90 percent of the soy sauce turned out in China.

"About 90 percent of Chinese soy sauce takes only about 3 weeks to make," said Nogi. While it is naturally brewed, the fermentation process takes only about 20 days, resulting in a soy sauce with no or very little alcohol content. Production of Kikkoman's soy sauce, on the other hand, is much more complex and requires a fermentation period of several months. The result is a much more complex product with a distinct aroma and taste, as well as a 2 percent alcohol content.

"I have heard through interviews that another 10 percent of Chinese soy sauce is made almost the same way as Japanese shoyu, except for one critical difference," said Nogi.

Instead of using indoor fermentation tanks in which the temperature of a wet mash called *moromi* is precisely controlled by computer, most Chinese soy sauce makers place their fermentation tanks outside of the building and allow its contents to be exposed to the sun. While this ancient method requires much less technology and is about as natural as you can get, it is less precise than the Japanese method.

"This soy sauce costs maybe two to three times as much as all other Chinese soy sauce," said Nogi. "So the market for it is very limited." One reason for this is the fact that Chinese-style soy sauce includes caramel.

Kikkoman's plans in China are not to flood the market with soy sauce. Instead, it plans to go after the upscale consumer. That means Kikkoman will target a small percentage of the Chinese market.

"Those at the higher income levels in China prefer Kikkoman quality, and we can supply that market," Nogi said.

In Taipei, says Kenzaburo Mogi, soy sauce consumption has, as in Japan, remained fairly flat for the past two decades. However, Kikkoman learned early on that demand for Japanese-style naturally brewed soy sauce was growing. But it learned something else, too—something that may eventually pay off for the much larger mainland Chinese market. While aficionados in Japan may prefer the traditionally brewed shoyu that Kikkoman has become famous for, Chinese palates are much different when it comes to soy sauce.

"We did some extensive market research to see what kind of soy sauce was the best seller in Taiwan," said Mogi.

The results revealed that even though demand for naturally brewed soy sauce was climbing in Taiwan, the kind of naturally brewed soy sauce that 90 percent of Taiwan's predominantly Chinese consumers wanted was a sweeter tasting variety than the type favored in Japan and the United States.

"This is a darker color soy sauce that has caramel coloring and sugar added," said Mogi. "They use it not only for flavor, but to darken the color of some foods."

While Kikkoman could produce this type of soy sauce, it was nevertheless faced with a problem.

"Everyone eventually agreed that we should create a customized product for Taiwan, but we couldn't really use the same label on this soy sauce that we use on our traditional product," said Mogi.

The result is a special label that indicates the contents have been sweetened with sugar.

"We only add sugar—no other chemicals," said Mogi. "That way we can keep 'naturally brewed' on the label."

Japanese shoyu purists are quite likely appalled by this kind of tampering with a product that many believe is humankind's most perfect condiment. But in business as in politics, it pays to be pragmatic about such things.

"We should make local products for local markets," said Mogi. "If local people in Taiwan prefer sweet, black color soy sauce, we should make it."

The same goes for other markets. In Korea, for example, that might mean making a Kikkoman version of *kanjyan*, Korea's traditional seasoning; in Thailand, it might be *nam pla*; in Vietnam, *nuoc maum*; and in Indonesia, *kecap manis* or *kecap asin*.

As Kikkoman prepares to enter the Chinese market, it has learned some interesting things about what kind of soy sauce it should make in China. For example, it learned that the northern part of China prefers regular, unadulterated Kikkoman Soy Sauce, while the southern part of the country prefers the sweetened, darker color product.

Because most Chinese soy sauce manufacturers are local companies that make their product for local markets, there is no true national brand in China. This is not necessarily by choice. In the past, China's ill-developed infrastructure, including an inadequate highway system, simply was not able to support nationwide shipments of products by truck. So shipping soy sauce from Beijing to Guangzhou, for example, was not always a viable option. With China embarked on a steady upgrade of its infrastructure, including rail, telecommunications, highways, and bridges, the opportunity to efficiently ship products from one end of China to another is becoming more feasible.

Once Kikkoman begins producing in China, its soy sauce could become China's first national brand of soy sauce, a Chinese economist in Washington, D.C., predicted. It's a bold prediction, but certainly not outrageous.

"Some people may find it strange that a product first created in China thousands of years ago should return to China with a Japanese label, but this is the way the global economy is supposed to work," said Arthur Chin, a consulting economist specializing on investment in China.

Of course, he added, there is no guarantee Kikkoman will become China's first national brand in soy sauce.

Shichiroemon Mogi, the First President of Kikkoman Corp. Shichiroemon Mogi was born in 1860 at Noda City, Chiba Prefecture. By succession he became the 6th Shichiroemon Mogi. He established the first laboratory in the industry in 1887, and made a great contribution to the innovations in the production technology of soy sauce. Mr. Mogi was selected as the first President of Noda Shoyu Co., Ltd., in 1917, and served until his death in 1929 at age 70.

Officers and directors of the Noda Shoyu Company gather in 1917. Note the early telephone and the gentleman at the left, the first Keizaburo Mogi, holding an abacus. The first president, Shichiroemon Mogi, is fifth from right.

The kakioke *(buckets) and* kaibo *(paddles) were some of the tools used in the past in making soy sauce.*

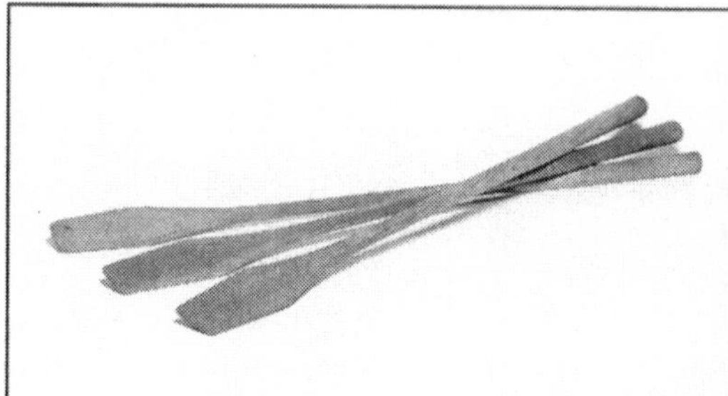

The Goyogura plant was built in Noda in 1939 to preserve the traditional techniques and equipment of soy sauce making. Production continues today to provide special soy sauce to Japan's Imperial household.

This automatic rotary machine, which greatly increased productivity, was developed in August 1930.

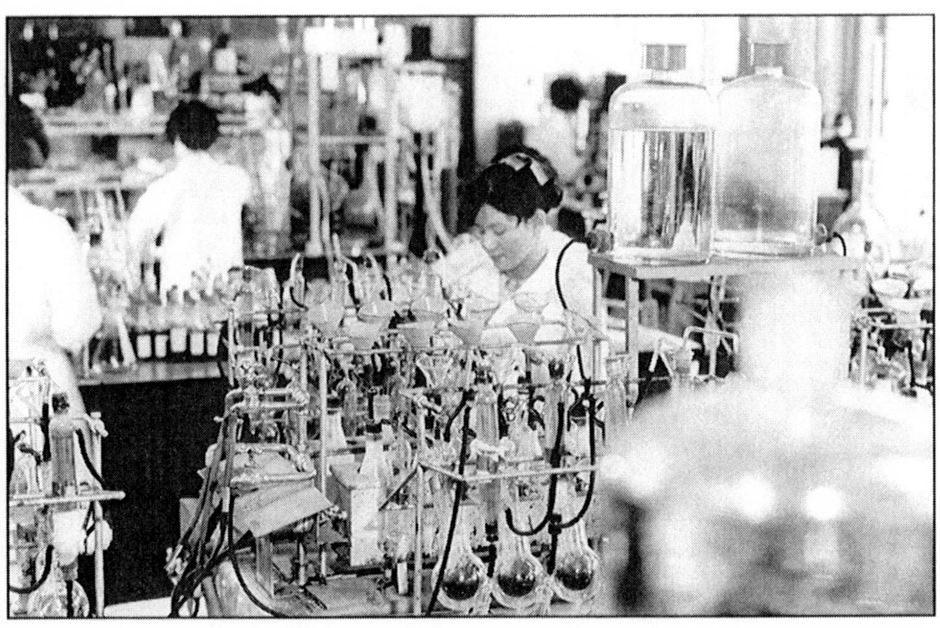

A laboratory in 1967 showing the process of analysis of nitrogen using the Kjeldahl method. The analysis determines the quality of soy sauce according to the level of nitrogen content creating "umami," or richness.

Various types of advertising were used by the Kikkoman Company throughout the years. The Good Housekeeping *seal of approval was adopted for the Kikkoman label in the U.S.A. The company expanded overseas, with a major base in the United States of America. In the beginning, soy sauce and teriyaki sauce were major products for overseas markets. Barbecue sauce and Menmi (soup base) were added to the original product line. In 1966, Japanese sake and plum wine were included.*

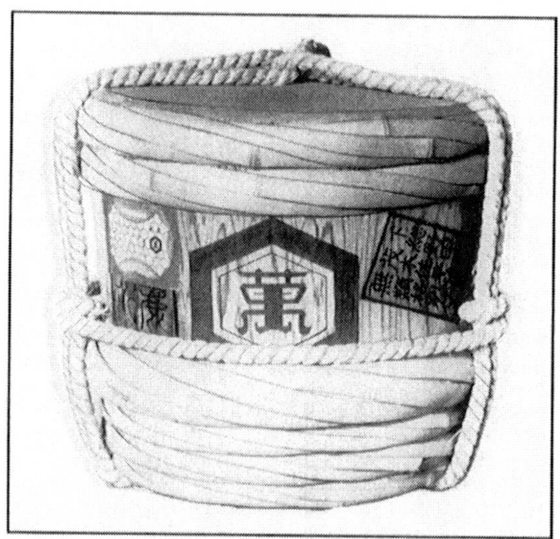

Barrels used for soy sauce were often decorated with emblems and branded seals (front and left). This barrel was in use around 1910 by the Saheiji Mogi family. The Kikkoman emblem was later adopted as the company trademark.

Soy beans and roasted, crushed wheat are mixed with a Kikkoman microorganism to make koji, a dry mash. The koji is kept in an environment of carefully controlled temperature and humidity to achieve optimum characteristics for the brewing process.

A workman checks a tank of moromi, the wet mash that is left in these fermentation tanks until the full flavor of soy sauce is achieved. One tank of moromi is enough to produce 20,000 one-liter bottles of soy sauce.

After the fermentation tanks, the moromi is poured into a very long cloth, folded over and pressed. The liquid now resembles soy sauce but must undergo heat treatment and other processing.

Kikkoman's computerized labeling equipment can run at various speeds and handle different size containers.

The Grand Opening of Kikkoman's plant in Walworth, Wisconsin, in June 1973 brought together a host of dignitaries for a joint ribbon-cutting ceremony. From left, William McConkey, deputy director of the U.S. Department of Commerce, Kikkoman President Keizaburo Mogi, Wisconsin Governor Patrick Lucey, Japanese Ambassador Nobuhiko Ushiba and Kikkoman Senior Managing Director Saheiji Mogi.

Kikkoman's first U.S. plant in Walworth, Wisconsin

The groundbreaking ceremony for Kikkoman's second U.S. plant in Folsom, California, was held in March 1997. Taking part in the ceremony were, from left, Folsom Mayor Glenn Fait, Yuzaburo Mogi, President and CEO of Kikkoman Corporation, Governor Pete Wilson of California and Kiyohiko Nanao, Consul General of Japan.

Mr. Yuzaburo Mogi, President and CEO of Kikkoman Corporation, Dutch Trade Minister Mrs. Anneke van Dok-van Weele, and Mrs. Yuzaburo Mogi gather for groundbreaking ceremonies on April 15, 1996, for Kikkoman's first soy sauce plant in Europe, near Groningen in The Netherlands.

Mr. Yuzaburo Mogi takes part in the Shinto ceremony during the groundbreaking in The Netherlands. At right is the Dutch Shinto priest who conducted the ceremony.

The Kikkoman story is one that begins in the narrow feudalism of 17th Century Japan when the ancestors of the current President and CEO Yuzaburo Mogi were engaged in soy sauce production using many workers. Kikkoman has since evolved into a global company far removed from the industry that grew up in rural Japan.

"There are other Japanese manufacturers, after all," Chin said. "And of course, it is entirely possible that a Chinese company may achieve this goal first."

When Kikkoman International, Inc., (KII), was formed as a joint investment in 1957 with Pacific Trading Co. of San Francisco, an import marketing company founded in 1911, the only well-developed U.S. soy sauce market was in California. JFC International, a major Oriental food distributor, was purchased by Kikkoman in 1969 along with a sister company called Taiheiyo Boeki Kabushiki Kaisha, or Pacific Trading Co. of Japan. JFC had developed a broad network of retail stores throughout California.

As Kikkoman was soon to learn, the sale of food products in the United States differs greatly from the tightly knit, highly centralized distribution system of Japan. For one thing, the U.S. system relies heavily on so-called food brokers whose job is to champion products to wholesalers and retailers. Kikkoman had its work cut out for it back in the 1950s. Few, if any, American food brokers had any idea what soy sauce was or how to use it. Consequently, promoting the product with wholesalers and retailers could not be accomplished without some hefty training.

And that's what Kikkoman did. KII worked long and hard at educating American food brokers about soy sauce. But it wasn't an overnight success. In fact, it took several years of sponsoring dinners and other events throughout California before Kikkoman landed its first major broker. That company, Mailliard & Schmiedell, represented Kikkoman products in California and eventually took over the seven main markets in the West.

The success or failure of a food broker is measured by his or her ability to convince wholesalers and retailers to carry certain products and then to display them conspicuously. To do that, the broker has to have a solid understanding of the product and how to use it.

According to industry insiders, education doesn't stop with the broker. It continues with the distributor, runs through the retailer, restaurant operator, or institutional user, and ends ultimately at the consumer, who also must be schooled about the product.

"After you convince brokers that a certain product is worth promoting, you have to educate them about how to use it," said a former Chicago food broker who agreed to discuss the system in return for anonymity.

"Food brokers in America have a lot of power," he continued. "They probably have too much power. They are really middlemen who control lots of shelf space in supermarkets. They and their sales people have to be convinced that the product is worth pushing. That means manufacturers like Kikkoman, who have products that aren't that familiar to the average white bread broker, have to spend a lot of time and money on so-called education.

"What that really means is that they have to offer incentives such as special promotions, contests, and other freebies as bait to get brokers to bite," he said. "Then they have to sponsor training programs for their products. These can include everything from simple golf outings to Caribbean cruises and foreign trips.

"In Kikkoman's case, you had a product that most mainstream Americans weren't familiar with back in the 1950s, so it really had its work cut out for it," he added. "But look at Kikkoman now. When you walk through a supermarket anywhere in America or go to any good restaurant—Oriental or otherwise—you would think that Kikkoman Soy Sauce has been part of mainstream America for 100 years. They've done a hell of a job."

The company knew it would have to approach America's Caucasian consumers differently than its Asian-American consumers. For example, before 1957, most Kikkoman Soy Sauce in the United States was sold in half-gallon cans or in larger tins. There was a logic to this. Most first- and second-generation Asian-American consumers tended to use greater amounts of soy sauce than their Caucasian counterparts, especially in cooking.

When Kikkoman decided to sell its soy sauce to the American mainstream, marketing research showed that few non-Asian Americans would buy a half-gallon tin of soy sauce at one time. Instead, they preferred their soy sauce in smaller glass bottles. It was the correct decision. And by the mid-1960s, just about every American could recognize Kikkoman's distinctive red-capped dispenser bottle.

But something else happened in the mid-1960s. Kikkoman introduced its Teriyaki Marinade & Sauce, which is made from soy sauce. It was a major marketing coup for Kikkoman because, at the time, there were no other soy sauce-based products available in the U.S. market. Twenty years later, Kikkoman introduced its *gen-en*, or low-sodium Lite Soy Sauce, which contains about 40 percent less salt than regular soy sauce.

Today, with Asian restaurants and recipes proliferating as never before in the history of American cuisine, Kikkoman is faced with a new challenge, says Chief Executive Yuzaburo Mogi. "To win continuously in the U.S. market, we must develop new products and new business," said Mogi. "The keywords for our company as we head into the next century are *challenge* and *innovation*."

To meet this vital challenge of innovation and to gather information and reinforce product development, Mogi moved a unit from San Francisco to Chicago in April 1997 and called it Kikkoman Marketing and Planning, or simply KMP. The unit, under the leadership of Kuniki Hatayama, vice president and treasurer of Kikkoman Foods, Inc. (KFI), is responsible for coordinating new product development between KFI (the subsidiary which oversees Kikkoman's Walworth and Folsom operations) and Kikkoman International, Inc. (the company's San Francisco-based marketing arm).

When KII was established in San Francisco, its primary purpose was to function as Kikkoman's sales and marketing arm in the United States. KFI, meanwhile, which was set up in 1972 as the operating company for the Walworth plant, would be Kikkoman's independent manufacturing arm. Kikkoman's leaders were convinced that the two disciplines required vastly different skills and that each needed to have a certain amount of freedom and authority to carry out their jobs.

But they also felt that creating a healthy sense of competition between the two American units would ultimately make both stronger as they competed with outside rivals. That internal competition would manifest itself as KII pushed KFI to provide adequate supplies of high-quality soy sauce at lower prices. It would also demand better packaging and bottling and quick delivery to customers. KFI, meanwhile, would put pressure on KII to sell more product so it could reduce costs through increased efficiencies created by higher production volume.

JFC International, Inc., would also function as an independent entity. JFC, which is the largest importer and distributor of Asian food products in the United States, sometimes competes with KII. For example, it sells Kikkoman Soy Sauce and other Kikkoman products on a nonexclusive basis. That means, in addition to Kikkoman products, it also handles products made by Kikkoman's competitors. But there are two sides to that coin. Even though Kikkoman sells soy sauce to JFC, it also sells to other U.S. wholesalers and brokers—a fact which keeps JFC on its toes.

Some may find this kind of internal competition disruptive or even hazardous. But not in a culture of selective risk. The fact that Kikkoman has moved its marketing and planning unit from San Francisco to Chicago indicates that it still believes firmly in the idea of internal competition. KMP will be pushed hard by KII, KFI, and JFC to come up with new products for the U.S. market.

Not long after KMP was moved, Kikkoman's Walworth facility began turning out its newest product—a new Roasted Garlic Teriyaki Marinade & Sauce. Another new product, Kikkoman Gourmet Sauce, was also launched. The new products contain various flavors and spices. While KMP can't take credit for the new products, which were conceived and developed in coordination with KII, it nevertheless will learn from their success or failure.

However, the first problem facing KMP's Hatayama was to find the right mix of people for the Chicago unit.

"We have a lot of technical people at Kikkoman, but they are not really that experienced when it comes to thinking up new products," Hatayama said. "This will be a big challenge for us. We will have to learn more about American eating habits."

One has a feeling that Shinzaburo Mogi would know exactly what Hatayama means. During his early one-man foray into the American market, Mogi faced more than his fair share of challenges. While his was an uphill battle at a time when many Americans were still only one or two generations removed from their European roots, the American consumers Kikkoman are dealing with are much more global in their tastes. That fact was recognized in the marketing strategy report prepared by Kaichiro Someya in 1995.

"Streets are overflowing with terms that show the current trend in the food product market," he wrote. "Ethnic foods, natural foods, healthy foods, gourmet foods, fancy foods, nutritious foods, weight watching foods, vegetarian foods, etc. In [Kikkoman's] attempt to match the consumer's likes and dislikes, diversification is steadily going forward."

Just how that diversification will manifest itself over the next several years in the U.S. market will depend on how Kikkoman marketing and planning rises to the challenge presented by Yuzaburo Mogi. Mogi, who is quick to point out that Kikkoman has not really developed any new major product for the U.S. market since the 1960s, says his challenge is to change Kikkoman's character.

"Kikkoman is a combination of the old and new," Mogi said. "Soy sauce, a traditional seasoning, connotes conservativeness. At the same time, it's related to biotechnology—one of the most promising high-tech areas for us in the twenty-first century. We will have to be much more aggressive in the future than we have been in the past in developing new products for the U.S. market."

Does that mean Kikkoman will be going head-to-head with some of America's food-processing giants? Not at all, says Mogi.

"I have no intention of competing with huge American food companies. We just want people to understand that we are an innovative international company that attaches great importance to the quality of its products."

"Making soy sauce is a bit like making iron," adds Yoshikuni Kato, a management consultant with A. T. Kearney in Tokyo.

"There is a long lead time from the raw materials to the end product," Kato said. "Iron needs to be strong, but to remain competitive, you have to introduce speed to the process."

It's a bit like sumo wrestling, Japan's true national sport. To the uninitiated, sumo appears to be nothing more than two extremely obese men pushing and shoving one another around a small round ring. Eventually, one stumbles and falls, and the match is over.

But sumo is much more complex than that. While sumo wrestlers are behemoths compared with most average Japanese, they are far from being the fat, flabby, uncoordinated grapplers whom those who don't understand the sport see. Years of harsh and sometimes brutal training result in wrestlers who are not only huge, but incredibly strong and surprisingly agile and swift on their feet. Sumo wrestlers are graded by a powerful professional sumo organization and only promoted from the lower ranks once they show a consistent ability to win.

It's a lot like producing something for the marketplace. Consumers judge products by their quality, utility, and price. Survival depends on consistently performing up to the consumers' expectations. Mogi, an avid sumo fan, says there are four lessons that business can learn from the world of sumo.

"The first lesson is that there is a big difference between a professional and an amateur," Mogi said. "Unlike a lot of sports, it takes a lot of time to become a champion in sumo. In baseball, on the other hand, a good pitcher in high school can become a good professional pitcher right away. We businessmen should be professionals."

But being a professional requires time. Just as a sumo wrestler needs time to learn the nuances, tactics, and strategies of sumo, businesspeople can only be considered professionals once they have learned the intricacies of the business world.

"The second lesson," Mogi continued, "is training. This is very important. Sumo wrestlers get up very early in the morning and go through rigorous training all morning. In that way, they become strong not only in body, but in mind."

Businesspeople must cultivate this type of discipline, he insists.

"The third lesson that business can learn from sumo is that in order to be successful, a sumo wrestler must develop some specialty—some methodology that he can use to defeat opponents," Mogi said.

For example, some sumo wrestlers specialize in speed, some specialize in pulling techniques, and some use powerful thrusts.

"You need a specialty in the sumo world to be strong and it's the same in business," he said.

Finally, there is the fourth lesson: The sumo world is basically free. While a sumo wrestler must be more than 173 cm (5 ft 7 in) tall and weigh more than 75 kg (165 lb), there are no restrictions on a sumo wrestler's upper limits. He can be as tall or as heavy as he wants. His only responsibility is to win.

"It's the same in business," said Mogi. "Real power is found in free competition. If a sumo wrestler loses, he cannot blame anyone. It is his responsibility. But in the business world, if a company fails, the chief executive often blames other people. That is wrong."

9 CHAPTER

High-Tech Fireflies and a Trailblazing Orange

Not far from where the founding ancestors of today's Kikkoman Corporation began brewing soy sauce in farmhouses more than 300 years ago stands a four-story battleship-gray building. From the outside, it's a rather unexceptional structure. But there is nothing unexceptional about what's going on inside this building located in the heart of Japan's Noda City just northeast of Tokyo. Here, rooms filled with DNA thermocyclers, Perkin-Elmer centrifuges, specialized fermentation tanks, spectrometers, infrared analyzers, and a broad array of other scientific instruments are being used to conduct experiments in biotechnology and genetic engineering that, at first glance, seem light-years away from soy sauce.

But are they?

"Making shoyu is really practicing the art of biotechnology," said Dr. Shigetaka Ishii, director of Kikkoman's research and development division. "In fact, soy sauce is actually one of man's oldest biotechnology products."

Indeed, research by the Soyfoods Center of Lafayette, California, reveals that some 2300 years ago a fermented forerunner of soy sauce was made in China as a preservative for meat and fish. And while what the world knows today as soy sauce wasn't produced in large quantities in Japan until the seventeenth century, it has nevertheless spawned volumes of data that scientists working in the field of biotechnology are using today. For example, Dr. Ishii points out that for more than 300 years Kikkoman has used a proprietary yeast and lactic bacteria to make the proprietary living microorganism or mold culture necessary to produce naturally brewed soy sauce. Using knowledge acquired from Kikkoman's microorganism, dozens of biotech products have been created.

While naturally brewed soy sauce is made by mixing together three main ingredients—soybeans, wheat, and salt—there is much more to it than that. Making soy sauce is a fermentation process requiring tiny living organisms such as Kikkoman's special mold culture, yeasts, and lactobacillus. It's a process in which proteins are converted to amino acids. The conversion of proteins in soybeans into amino acids occurs at the same time that roasted wheat is digesting the mold or "seed starter" culture. This yields a richer tasting sauce. The roasted wheat "digests" the culture and produces more enzymes, which in turn enhance the aroma of soy sauce. Finally, the soy sauce is pasteurized, which stabilizes it.

It's a process that required early shoyu brewers to possess an intuitive, if not scientific, understanding of biotechnology and microbiology. Over the years, as Kikkoman Soy Sauce brewers became more and more familiar with the microorganisms that are necessary for producing naturally brewed soy sauce, they began to understand the technology better. Among other things, they learned how to compress the time needed to produce soy sauce.

In the midseventeenth century, when the first Mogi and Takanashi families began brewing soy sauce and *miso* (fermented soybean paste) just down the road from Kikkoman's research and development center, they needed at least 1 year to produce an acceptable product. Today, by introducing modern production techniques, that 1 year has been reduced to several months. But even more important than reducing the cycle time for soy sauce production is the promise that biotechnology and genetic engineering hold for Kikkoman as it enters the twenty-first century.

Kikkoman President and CEO Yuzaburo Mogi has declared that creating new products based on the company's biotechnology competencies is one of his long-term strategies.

"Investment in this area is high," Mogi said. "Two thirds of our R&D investment is going into biotechnology."

In 1996, biotechnology and genetic engineering accounted for a little more than 1 percent of Kikkoman's sales, according to Katsumi Ishizuka, deputy general manager of Kikkoman's biochemicals division. Yuzaburo Mogi is not satisfied with that, however. His target is for Kikkoman's biotech revenue to grow to 10 percent of 1996 domestic sales by the year 2005. Mogi is also calling for biotech to provide Kikkoman with one third of its profits by 2005. To do that, Kikkoman, considered a pioneer in developing somatic hybrid plants and genetic engineering, will continue its research into new diagnostic pharmaceuticals, the technology of screening microbes, the technology of enzyme production, recombinant genetic engineering, and cell-fusion technology.

It's a strategy that makes a lot of sense. For one thing, profits on biotech products are higher than on soy sauce and the company's other traditional products. But there is another reason for setting this goal. Using centuries of traditional fermentation prowess and expertise—including a deep understanding of enzymes and microorganisms—as a launching pad, Kikkoman has already developed more than 250 products for the pharmaceutical, medical diagnostic, and food-processing industries since it was awarded its first biotech patent in 1977. These include a lineup of industrial, pharmaceutical, and diagnostic enzymes and microorganisms that have sprung from what Ishizuka calls "old, classical biotech."

As with other companies that have entered the sometimes exotic world of biotechnology, Kikkoman's successes in genetic engineering are an outgrowth of pioneering breakthrough research done by scientists as far back as 1869, when German biochemist Friedrich Miescher first discovered the existence of deoxyribonucleic acid, or DNA. DNA conveys the codes of genetic information that transmit inherited characteristics to successive generations of plants and animals.

In 1943, DNA's role in inheritance was demonstrated, and in 1953, American biochemist James D. Watson and English physicist Francis H. C. Crick were able to determine its structure by clarifying the chemical makeup and molecular arrangement of genes. Specifically, Watson and Crick were able to demonstrate that genes were long double-helix molecules of DNA. For their trailblazing work in genetics, Watson and Crick received the Nobel Prize in physiology in 1962. But even more important, their work opened the way for the direct manipulation of genetic material rather than reliance on traditional methods of selective breeding and hybridization—a critical development for companies like Kikkoman that produced food products.

In 1973, American researchers added to that body of knowledge by conducting the first successful experiments in splicing foreign genetic material into a living organism's DNA. Then they were able to observe how the new gene was expressed in succeeding generations of that organism. By 1976, this "gene-splicing" technology (also known as "recombinant DNA formation") was already beginning to spill from the scientific laboratory to the business world. As it had been with other technologies in the past, Kikkoman was first out of the blocks. Its first gene-splicing patent was in 1977, the first ever issued in Japan.

The perceived commercial potential of biotechnology swept through companies in Japan and elsewhere like a tsunami. In 1980, the government of Japan declared that biotechnology was a key basic future technology that Japan must master by the turn of the century. By 1981, the optimistic fervor created by the promise of biotechnology caused the number of Japanese companies involved in biotechnology research and development to explode from a handful to more than 150, including Kikkoman Corporation.

However, a decade later, it was painfully obvious to many companies that creating products from biotechnology was a bit more complex and expensive than they had estimated. The high costs associated with developing products via biotechnology often resulted in products with little or no commercial viability. They were either too expensive or they took too long to get from laboratory to marketplace. And simply throwing money and people at the problem was no antidote. Many companies found that they didn't have the proper corporate culture to successfully spur efforts in biotechnology. They either lacked the creativity and know-how necessary to develop new products or they lacked the staying power and long-term vision required to bring products from the lab to the consumer.

That wasn't a problem at Kikkoman, however. With more than 300 years of experience in biotechnology, Kikkoman was well-positioned to take advantage of the new breakthroughs in recombinant DNA technology. For centuries, the forerunners of today's Kikkoman Corporation had worked with enzymes as they steadily improved the biochemical and fermentation processes needed to produce naturally brewed shoyu.

The term *enzyme* is derived from a Greek word meaning "in yeast." And though the word was first coined in 1878, people have made use of enzymes for thousands of years. Their structure, the reactions they promote, and how they function as catalysts have all been a critical part of brewing beer, fermenting wine, and baking bread—some of our oldest known commercial activities.

Enzymes are the critical catalysts within a cell that promote the chemical reactions necessary for life. They catalyze the formulation of DNA, RNA, phospholipids, sugars, polysaccharides (found in plant starch and animal glycogen), fatty acids, and proteins, among other things. The men and women who produced fermented soy sauce in Japan knew intuitively—if not scientifically—just how important enzymes were. They knew that they speeded up a host of chemical reactions, including oxidation, hydrolysis, and synthesis. But most important, they knew that enzymatic activity was necessary to produce naturally brewed soy sauce.

For much of Kikkoman's history, that's all that counted. Producing top-quality soy sauce was, after all, the company's key competence. But in the 1960s and 1970s, that began to change with domestic consumption of soy sauce leveling off and even declining. If Kikkoman could utilize the new breakthroughs in genetic engineering and biotechnology to develop its knowledge of enzymes and microorganisms, it might be able to offset the flatness in the soy sauce market by developing new products. That's exactly what it did, says Ishizuka.

"The soy sauce business leveled off in Japan about 40 years ago," he said. "By 1955, the domestic market was saturated. One way to keep the company alive and growing was to go abroad with our product, which we did. Another way was through diversification, and the result of that was Mann's Wines and Nippon Del Monte." But another way was to exploit the company's expertise in biotechnology. In 1961, Kikkoman researchers discovered enzymes that could be developed into digestive aids, recalls Ishizuka.

"Our researchers found that these enzymes were effective in high-level acid such as is found in the stomach," Ishizuka said.

In 1962, Kikkoman set up a separate company called Seishin Pharmaceuticals to develop and market products based on the company's enzyme technology. It didn't take Kikkoman long to introduce two new enzyme products to the pharmaceutical industry. Molsin, an acid-stable protease, and Stalase, an acid stable amylase, were soon being supplied to pharmaceutical companies as a raw material for digestive-aid products.

Cyclic AMP, which is used in making drugs designed to treat skin disorders and bedsores, and Gallic acid, which is used to make antioxidants, inks, dyes, ultraviolet absorption chemicals, and thermographic paper as well as various products for the pharmaceutical and semiconductor industries, soon followed.

Within 6 years, Kikkoman began marketing diagnostic enzymes and substrates to companies such as a large photo film producer in the U.S. and a pharmaceutical manufacturer in Germany. Kikkoman's proprietary diagnostic enzymes run the gamut of more than 17 products from those such as Sarcosine oxidase and Uricase, which are used to test kidney functions, to Maltopentaose and its derivatives and Glucosidase, which are used to test the function of the pancreas.

The company has also created a lineup of six industrial enzymes. Tannase, which reduces sediment in tea, is used by customers such as a large tea company. There is also Pectolyase, a clarifying enzyme that is used by food processors to keep fruit juice clear.

Chlorogenic acid esterase, which controls bitterness and prevents enzymatic browning in fruit and plants, is used in the processing of juice, wine, and in the production of coffee beverages.

In 1997, Kikkoman was marketing 12 research reagents and kits for the food-processing and cosmetic industries. A reagent is a substance that is used to detect or measure another substance or to convert one substance into another by means of the reaction it causes.

The company also has two significant products under development. KPA-40®, a grape seed extract, is used as an antitoxicant by industrial customers and the health food industry as an antiaging agent. Among other things, it prevents oxidation and discoloration in a wide range of food products, from processed fish and meat to vitamins, drinks, candy, seasonings, and milk products. So far, more than 20 patents are pending in Japan and other countries for the product.

Another product under development by Kikkoman is Isoflavon®, an estrogen for women that is extracted from soybeans. This new soybean-based product helps women during the aging process by strengthening bone structure and is a prime example of how Kikkoman is using its ancient knowledge of soybeans and enzymes to create new products for the twenty-first century.

One of Kikkoman's brightest successes is, ironically, related to light. Specifically, it involves the light emitted by the tiny firefly (*hotaru*), an insect that has strong mythological and literary significance in Japanese history.

In *The Tale of Genji,* Japan's most famous work of fiction written in the eleventh century, one of the key characters in the story catches his first glimpse of the Lady Tamakazura by the light of fireflies. There are other stories of poor scholars in China studying by the light of fireflies during the summer.

In ancient Japan, it was thought that the spirits of warriors who had met a tragic death assumed the form of a firefly, according to the *Kodansha Encyclopedia of Japan.* Others believed that the light emitted by fireflies were the souls of the dead. During Japan's Edo period (1600–1868), firefly watching became a common summer pastime. Woodblock prints of the era depict Japanese dressed in light summer *kimono* or *yukata* and carrying *uchiwa* (round fans) gathering along the Sumida River in Tokyo or sitting in special firefly-viewing boats on the Uji River in Kyoto or at Ishiyama on the shores of Lake Biwa.

Watching fireflies may be a relaxing way to spend an evening, but researchers at Kikkoman had something else in mind. The soft, glowing light emitted by a firefly is created when the luciferase enzyme, which is produced by the insect, mingles with a substance known as adenosine triphosphate (ATP) and oxidizes molecules of a pigment called luciferin.

For years, scientists have used luciferase in gene-splicing experiments. In one such experiment, the gene that produces the luciferase enzyme was transferred to a tobacco plant. When the roots of the plant were immersed in a solution containing the same chemical ingredients carried by the firefly, the tobacco plant began to emit light.

This proved that plant cells can serve as recipients of animal genes. But it led to other more immediately practical uses. For example, scientists found that luciferase can be used to detect harmful microorganisms that can be disastrous for hospitals, food-processing plants, and even semiconductor factories where microorganism-free "clean rooms" are essential.

It's a similar technique that scientists have used to test for life on the moon and other planets in our solar system. Because all life forms contain ATP, the luciferase test will detect all microorganisms, including harmful ones borne by water. When it does, the luciferase "lights up" in the same way that a firefly glows. It's a foolproof test. The problem is its cost.

"It takes more than 30,000 fireflies to yield just 1 g of the luciferase enzyme," said Shinichi Sugiyama, president of Nippon Del Monte Corporation and former managing director of Kikkoman's research and development division. "Extracting and processing natural luciferase is expensive—about $70,000 per gram. That's too expensive for broad commercial use."

Kikkoman researchers, combining centuries of enzyme expertise with the latest ideas in gene splicing, found a way around that problem. Researchers in Kikkoman's biotechnology division succeeded in mass-producing luciferase in 1987 using recombinant DNA technology. While the new product was more stable than natural luciferase taken from fireflies, it nevertheless deteriorated in a few minutes at room temperature. That made it unsuitable for commercial applications.

Kikkoman has since improved on this process with a new thermostable luciferase, a fact which Ishizuka says has made Kikkoman number one in the market. It's a six-step process that begins with the isolation of a copy of the luciferase gene taken from the lantern cells of the firefly. The gene is then synthesized and the blueprint integrated into the *Escherichia coli* (*E. coli*) chromosome via a proprietary gene vector that Kikkoman has dubbed "sleeper." In biology, a vector is the transport DNA that carries the cloned DNA fragment to a microorganism such as *E. coli* during genetic manipulation. Kikkoman's sleeper vector allows scientists to control this process. In essence, the *E. coli* microorganism grows while the proprietary vector "sleeps," or is inactive at a lower temperature.

According to Kikkoman technical publications, when the microorganism is returned to its original state of 32°C after heating at 42° for 30 minutes, the vector "awakens" from its sleep and transmits or amplifies the transplanted blueprint to 500–1000 times the number of *E. coli* genes. The result is the production of the genetically engineered luciferase enzyme in large quantities at one time for a fraction of the cost of the natural product. It's a proprietary process that Kikkoman uses not only for the production of luciferase, but for the mass production of other diagnostic and research enzymes such as an enzyme for the detection of kidney conditions.

But there is another feature to Kikkoman's luciferase. The company has come up with portable testing instruments and Lumitesters—hand-held electronic devices that allow food processors to test for harmful microorganisms at any point along the food-processing line.

However, the use of Kikkoman's luciferase is not limited to the food-processing industry. Hospitals and semiconductor manufacturers are also using it and the company's lineup of testing equipment, as are other industries which use large quantities of water that must be continually monitored for contaminating microorganisms. For example, the paper and pulp manufacturing industry, brewers of beer, and firms that sell bottled drinking water are all potential users of Kikkoman's luciferase testing system. It's a market that Ishizuka says is expanding very rapidly.

"An American company forecasts a potential worldwide market for luciferase of 400 billion yen (about $3.3 billion)," said Ishizuka.

According to Kikkoman researchers, the company's luciferase is much more efficient than other testing agents and can produce accurate results with far fewer tests.

"And we don't have to harm any fireflies to do any of this," remarked one Kikkoman researcher, "because the luciferase is genetically engineered."

Kikkoman's safety testing facility in Noda, where toxicologists probe and examine the properties of food and the harmful microorganisms that can attack it, is one of the largest in Japan's food industry. As other companies that have poured money and talent into biotechnology and genetic engineering have learned, the investment can be time consuming. For example, on the top floor of Kikkoman's research facility, Dr. Asahi Matsuyama is part of a 10-year government-supported project to develop "supercells."

In effect, the project, which is partially funded by Japan's Ministry of International Trade and Industry and by Kikkoman, is designed to use gene manipulation technology to improve the production efficiency of microorganisms and to develop a revolutionary bioreactor system. The object is to place the production of protein and enzymes in cells under human control and thereby improve the efficiency of the process. "The idea is to reduce the time for fermentation by controlling the phases between the growth of the cell and the production of the enzyme," said Dr. Matsuyama. "That will allow us to reduce the time needed for fermentation in soy sauce and other products."

But Kikkoman isn't stopping with genetic engineering. Centuries of producing soy sauce have taught it some valuable lessons about the production of food and food products. The company's food engineers have developed a range of automated food-production machinery and other products for the food-processing industry. For example, there is a system that sterilizes powders and granules such as spices, nuts, and cereals using superheated steam instead of ethylene oxide gas, which has been reported to adversely affect some people. Then there is the *genmai* cooker, a device developed by Kikkoman that eliminates the need for pressure cooking. Kikkoman engineers have also developed the Kid's Cooker, a system that sterilizes viscous liquids by heating without causing significant deterioration of the liquid's quality.

In 1993, Kikkoman absorbed Seishin Pharmaceuticals to bring its critical biotechnology research arm into the company's mainstream and to get its researchers closer to the market, according to Ishizuka. With rapidly expanding global markets for genetically engineered and new biotech products, Kikkoman wants to be sure its expertise in the use of enzymes is leveraged to the fullest extent.

"Biochemicals have become the fifth division of Kikkoman Corporation, along with soy sauce, products related to soy sauce, wine and liquor, and Del Monte," Ishizuka pointed out.

Just outside the building where Kikkoman scientists are splicing genes is a collection of modest looking greenhouses. But there is nothing modest about the work going on inside them. Here, researchers like Dr. Toshifumi Ohgawara have managed to do something no one else has done. Using cell-fusion technology, they have produced a new orange that could not exist in nature.

The orange, called the *Oretachi,* is unique in that it can be grown in cold climates. What does this mean? Think about it. Most orange trees need the warm sun of places like California and Florida to thrive and produce fruit. Few will survive long in climates with any type of prolonged frost. But what if you could grow oranges in places like Minnesota and even Alaska, where frosts are prevalent and deadly to most citrus plants? Suddenly, you have agricultural opportunities that never existed before.

As with other citrus fruits, oranges are native to southern China and Southeast Asia, where they and other citrus fruits have been cultivated for some 4000 years. The first lemons, limes, oranges, and shaddocks were carried to eastern Africa and the Middle East sometime between A.D. 100 and 700, according to *Compton's Encyclopedia.* But mandarin oranges didn't arrive in Europe and the United States from Asia until the nineteenth century.

While the technology shows great promise, the Oretachi is still in the experimental stages and far from being a commercial product. But that hasn't stopped people like Dr. Ohgawara from continuing to experiment and dream. After all, just getting the Oretachi from the test tube to the tree is a remarkable accomplishment. As with other citrus fruits, it is extremely difficult to cross-breed, even between related species.

It was a 5-year process that began when the fused cells of a three-leaf trifoliate orange, which is able to withstand cold weather but which produces an inedible fruit, and a single-leaf Trovita orange were cultured in a liquid medium. A month later, the divided cell had grown to a mass of hundreds of cells. Not long thereafter, small globular embryoids were moved to a solid medium, and within 3 months, the embryoids had fully developed. Five months later, trifoliate hybrid plants were regenerated from these embryoids.

About a year after the fused cells were first combined, the regenerated somatic hybrids were transferred to pots where the plants began to grow. Five years later, the first Oretachi plant bore fruit. The plant itself bore characteristics of both parents. It had three leaves like the trifoliate orange, but those leaves were thicker and larger like those of the Trovita orange. Unfortunately, like the trifoliate orange, the Oretachi's fruit is not of commercial quality. But that's a problem that Dr. Ohgawara and other Kikkoman researchers are working on.

While the world is familiar with such hybrids as tangelos (tangerine and grapefruit) and tangors (sweet orange and tangerine), it has yet to be introduced to the Oretachi and the offshoots of the research that went into producing it. For example, using cell-fusion technology, Kikkoman has also produced a plant called a *Gravel,* which is a combination of grapefruit and navel orange, and a *Shiuvel,* a combination of unshiu mandarin orange and a navel orange.

Why bother with such things? If you are in the food business, you have to be constantly looking for new products to create and market, says Dr. Ishii. While the Gravel plant has yet to produce fruit, Kikkoman is intrigued with the idea of producing a new navel orange that has the taste of a grapefruit or a navel orange and can be easily peeled by hand like the unshiu mandarin orange.

"We are now working on a mandarin orange-lime fruit," said Dr. Ishii.

While it sounds like an intriguing combination, the objective is not just to introduce a new, strange-looking, different tasting orange to the market. Kikkoman has another agenda, one that is not far removed from the product that got it into the twentieth century.

"We want to produce a new fruit that will go well with soy sauce," Dr. Ishii said.

Given Kikkoman's centuries-long experience in using "old" biotechnology to make soy sauce, it follows that it should use gene splicing, cell fusion, or any other kind of scientific alchemy to perpetuate its core product while creating new ones. Yasuo Takeyama, former managing director in charge of the editorial board at Japan's *Nihon Keizai Shimbun* (the Japanese equivalent of *The Wall Street Journal*) and a man who has followed Kikkoman's passage into the global marketplace, agrees.

"Kikkoman is a very steady company, but it must continually look for new areas of business," Takeyama said. "Where will Kikkoman find this new area of business? Del Monte tomato products will not be enough. Nor will wine or even soy sauce. It will be biotech."

10 CHAPTER

Soy Sauce Meets Cyberspace:

Big Changes on the Road to the Twenty-first Century

On a bright winter day in February 1997, Yuzaburo Mogi walked to the podium of the World Economic Forum in Davos, Switzerland, gazed out over an audience of international economists, business leaders, and journalists, and began talking about the more than 300-year-old company he leads. It was another of those defining moments in a life that has been filled with them. Mogi had come not only to talk about Kikkoman, but about Japan.

As vice chairman of Japan's powerful *Keizai Doyukai* (Japan Association of Corporate Executives) and chairman of the Committee on Infrastructure for New Industries, Mogi was representing both company and country at the prestigious gathering. It was a tall order, but one that Mogi quickly demonstrated he was well-suited for. Even though Mogi comes from an ancient and traditional Japanese family, he is an internationalist at heart who understands the need to take risks.

But being a risktaker is only a part of what makes Mogi run. He is also a pragmatist—a man who understands that Japan, Kikkoman, and every other Japanese company can survive and thrive only if there is a free international marketplace where creativity and innovation, not protectionism and overregulation, are what determines success.

"In order to revitalize the Japanese economy," Mogi began, "we must learn from the experience of the United States in the 1980s."

It was a painful time in America, he told the audience. Many existing companies had to restructure and reengineer themselves to survive. Entire product lines were abandoned. Jobs were lost. The hue and cry were enormous, especially against Japan, which was perceived as the cause. But even as companies were consolidating or restructuring, new enterprises were emerging from the rubble and new markets were being created.

"Unemployment from the [U.S.] restructuring was covered by the labor needs of the new enterprises," Mogi continued. "In fact, there were more new jobs created by the new enterprises than those lost by the old restructured companies."

It's a model that Japan must follow, Mogi added. The Japanese economy is changing from one managed by bureaucrats to one driven by free competition and enterprise. Only companies that follow the path of innovation will survive in this new, rapidly maturing economic environment. Leaders of Japanese companies must place innovation at the top of the corporate value system.

Mogi could very well have been talking about his own company. As one of Japan's oldest (if not *the* oldest) continuously operated enterprises, Kikkoman is often regarded in Japan as a conservative company rich in tradition. But it also has been one of Japan's most innovative and assertive companies, especially since Yuzaburo Mogi was named president and CEO in 1995. It's a company that has consistently created new global markets for one of Japan's oldest and most traditional commercial products (naturally brewed soy sauce) by turning it from a uniquely Japanese product into a global "all-purpose seasoning" and by adapting it to different international palates. In addition, Kikkoman has devised entirely new soy sauce-based products for markets as diverse as the United States, Taiwan, and Brazil.

"If you stay with existing products and existing businesses, you can't expect much growth," he said.

Strong leadership at the top of a company is essential, Mogi added. You can't win in the new global economy without strong leaders who promote constant innovation. Nor can you depend on old systems of management—not even if they are Japanese—to lead you into the twenty-first century.

You need creative employees, not simply obedient employees. And these employees must be evaluated frequently. The Japanese idea of lifetime employment is not practical, at least in its current form. But the lifetime employment system has merit and should be adjusted to the myriad social and economic changes sweeping today's Japan. Old pyramidal types of organizations are not practical either. They tend to stifle rather than promote innovation, Mogi said. To accelerate innovation, a flat organization is necessary.

An organization, especially a large organization like Kikkoman, needs to be flexible. It needs to consist of more "project teams" that promote horizontal communication across departments. When that occurs, better vertical communication will follow. Japanese companies will also have to introduce a personnel management system that contains many more incentives and requires periodic assessments of employees, Mogi continued.

"Basically, in Japan, we still have the seniority system in which wage increases and promotions are based on age and term of service," Mogi told the audience. "It will be very difficult to change this system completely, but Japanese companies must try."

They must create more incentives or introduce merit-based pay scales designed to encourage better performance if they are to compete successfully, Mogi added. He has been trying to accomplish both since his appointment as CEO.

"In 1996, I introduced an incentive system for our general manager class," Mogi said.

But innovative management tools will not by themselves ensure survival, Mogi said. Japanese companies will need to energize their research and development departments as never before. One way to do this is to offer incentives to researchers who can quickly create viable new products that in turn will spawn new businesses. Again, while this is still a work in progress, Kikkoman is attempting to be an innovator in this critical area.

One of the first things Mogi did after he was named CEO was to create seven "product managers" in an effort to forge a stronger link between the consumer and Kikkoman's product development and production sectors. By using these product managers as a bridge between Kikkoman and its customers, Mogi hopes to reduce the amount of time it takes to get a product to market. But even more important is the need to make sure the products Kikkoman does produce are the ones its customers want and then to tailor those products accordingly.

Finally, contrary to all the hype about Japanese manufacturing and marketing prowess, Japanese companies cannot go it alone. They need to create strategic alliances with other companies. And a growing number of those alliances will be with foreign firms.

"I am not only talking about taking over other companies," Mogi said. "I am talking about cooperating with each other in order to develop new opportunities and innovative businesses. Acquisitions are another possibility."

Once again, Mogi was speaking from experience. In 1963, Kikkoman created a groundbreaking strategic alliance with America's California-based Del Monte Corporation that has become a stellar example in Japan of cooperation between a U.S. and a Japanese company. Not only has the alliance been lucrative for both companies, but it was a critical element in Kikkoman's move toward diversification. For example, the long-term relationship Kikkoman has had with Del Monte led to a 1990 perpetual rights agreement with the California company that gave Kikkoman exclusive rights to produce, package, and sell Del Monte brand products for Asia and the Pacific, except for the Philippines.

"Japan's market has become freer and more competitive," Mogi said. "But business is like war, and companies win or lose."

Mogi added, competition must be fair under rules that are part of a global standard.

"We have a Mogi family constitution that we have observed throughout the history of our company. Among other things, Article 11 of that constitution says: `True profit comes from hard work and maximum effort. Speculation is not the best road to follow. Business which is done contrary to social order and by taking advantage of others' weakness should be prohibited.'"

These were words that few in the audience had ever heard from the lips of a Japanese businessman. And when Mogi suggested Japan follow some elements of the U.S. model that helped pull the U.S. economy from the doldrums of the 1980s and early 1990s, some may have been a bit surprised. Mogi added that Japan could learn from the U.S. system of fostering venture businesses in order to regenerate industries and enterprises. Existing Japanese companies should also develop more new businesses, he said.

Such advice was much different from that heard 10 years before. After all, it was in the 1980s that much of the world had pronounced Japan the winner and the United States the loser in their economic *passage d'arms.* The U.S. economy was old, sputtering, and incapable of keeping up with the dynamic economies of Asia, led by Japan, many experts declared. American products were inferior in quality and American companies were not responsive to consumers. In contrast, the Japanese economy was young, vital, and explosive. Its products were world class and in great demand everywhere. Stand aside, Uncle Sam, here comes Nippon.

In fact, few knew it at the time, but Japan was riding the filmy crown of a bubble economy made ever more fragile by a grossly inflated real estate market, an undervalued yen, banks that were overextended with questionable loans, and an excessive dependence on exports for survival. Now, here was one of Japan's top business leaders essentially confirming what many skeptics of Japan's economic success had been saying all along: If Japan is going to consistently succeed, it will have to discard government overregulation and disavow or drastically adapt many Japanese business and financial practices to international standards.

One wonders if Mogi's ancestors were watching, and if so, what they must have been thinking. Here was one of their own—a man who grew up making soy sauce in the small town of Noda, Japan—talking to the world's business and political elite about international business and economics. When the first Mogis, led by an intrepid woman named Shige Maki, began brewing soy sauce in the mid-1600s, their knowledge of the world barely extended beyond the borders of Noda—the town some 30 mi north of Tokyo where Japan's shoyu industry began and still thrives. The Japan of the seventeenth century was a feudal, insular land closed to the outside world. The idea that Japanese shoyu would ever be consumed, let alone produced, in other countries was inconceivable. And the thought that someday a Mogi might be addressing a meeting in a far off place called Europe that the Japanese of the seventeenth century had only known about for a few decades was even more unthinkable.

Of course, could they have imagined Yuzaburo Mogi's career at Kikkoman, they would have known that his attendance at such international gatherings is not out of character for him. After all, Mogi is one of the most internationally minded businessmen in Japan. Not only was he the first Japanese to earn an MBA at Columbia University (1961), but he was also the person most responsible for convincing Kikkoman to build its first U.S. soy sauce plant (1972).

It is a pattern of international behavior that seems to permeate the Mogi bloodline. As far back as the midnineteenth century, when few people outside of Japan had even heard of Japanese soy sauce, let alone tasted it, the Mogi's were already aggressively marketing their product at world's fairs and other exhibitions in Europe, the United States, and throughout Asia.

In the past 50 years, Kikkoman has managed to take one of Japan's most traditional products and create a market for it in nearly 100 countries. In the United States alone, it commands a 50 percent market share of what Nielsen Market Research North America says is almost a $160-million "Oriental bottle sauce market." Even more impressive, however, is Kikkoman's annual U.S. growth rate. Between 1986 and 1996, Kikkoman's soy sauce production volume in the United States rose a staggering 2.6 times, representing an average annual increase of 10.1 percent, Mogi pointed out in the company's 1996 annual report. Globally, Kikkoman's 1997 production capacity of soy sauce hit an all-time high of 440,000 kL (116 million gal).

Even more significant were Kikkoman's overseas sales, which jumped 21.8 percent to 54.4 billion yen ($469 million) and accounted for 25.4 percent of consolidated net sales—up about 4.4 percentage points from fiscal 1995, Mogi said in the annual report. While the declining value of the Japanese yen helped boost overseas sales, the increase is also attributable to the performance of Kikkoman's U.S. subsidiaries.

When you consider that one of those U.S. subsidiaries (Kikkoman Foods, Inc., in Walworth, Wisconsin) would not have been around had it not been for Mogi's determination and tenacity in the early 1970s, it seems fitting that he be standing before some of the world's top business and political leaders in Davos talking about global business strategies, the sluggish Japanese economy, Japan's system of management, and trade relations. In fact, among Japan's top business leaders, Yuzaburo Mogi was a logical choice to be standing behind the podium. You don't get to be vice chairman of the *Keizai Doyukai* by being a shrinking violet.

Along with the *Keidanren* (Japan Federation of Economic Organizations), *Nikkeiren* (Japan Federation of Employers' Associations), and *Nissho* (Japan Chamber of Commerce and Industry), the Keizai Doyukai comprises Japan's so-called *Zaikai*—the power brokers who represent the nation's business and financial world. The Keizai Doyukai is one of the four pillars supporting modern industrial Japan. The meaning of the word *Zaikai* says it all. *Zai* means "money" and *kai* means "world."

Each of the four organizations, while private, nevertheless exerts tremendous influence on Japan's government and its economic policies. Individually, they represent the top management of Japan's major industrial corporations and financial institutions. Collectively, they are Japan's biggest champions of the capitalist system. But of all these groups, the 1500-member Keizai Doyukai is probably the most internationally minded. Most of its members are managing directors, chairmen, or presidents of major Japanese corporations. But even more important are the policies Keizai Doyukai supports and promotes—namely, liberalization of trade and capital in Japan and the lessening of trade friction with the United States and other nations.

It's an organization that Mogi seems perfectly suited to help lead. And Kikkoman is a company that many within the Keizai Doyukai have consistently benchmarked. Not only has the company been a leader in adopting new management methods, but it has been a pioneer in marketing products around the world—a fact not lost on other Japanese who have closely studied Kikkoman's march into new world markets and are continuing to observe it closely as it heads into the twenty-first century.

"Kikkoman is a joyful paradox," said "Maurie" Kaoru Kobayashi, professor of international management at Tokyo's Sanno Institute of Business Administration and Management. "It's an old, traditional company that is at the same time extremely innovative. It's a company with strong tradition and it is led by somebody [Mogi] who has inherited that tradition. But at the same time, Mogi is somebody who is capable of outbursts of energy and creativity. For that reason, Kikkoman is the best example of this joyful paradox in Japan today."

That "joyful paradox" began with television commercials for soy sauce in mid-1950s America and continued in the 1960s and 1970s with Kikkoman-owned restaurants in Europe which were used to introduce soy sauce and soy sauce-based products to new European consumers. While that may seem a logical thing to do today, 30 or 40 years ago it was revolutionary, said Yousuke Kinugasa, director of the Institute of International Business at Japan's Kanagawa University. Kikkoman was one of the first Japanese companies to understand the concept of product customization, Professor Kinugasa said.

"Kikkoman was aggressive in developing international products for international markets," he said. "For example, it made its Teriyaki Marinade & Sauce specifically for the U.S. market and it created Lite Soy Sauce for the international market. That demonstrated tremendous intuition and leadership."

That intuition and leadership were still alive and well on April 28, 1997, when Kikkoman launched an English-language version of its popular Internet home page on the World Wide Web. Kikkoman's new web page signaled yet another channel that the company is using to market its soy sauce and lineup of 2000 other products worldwide. The page (http://www.kikkoman.co.jp) contains more than 200 pages of information in English, and it experienced almost 30,000 hits during its first few weeks on the Web. In keeping with Kikkoman's international marketing strategy, the home page is presented as though it were a cookbook.

Profile contains basic background on the company along with financial data and investor relations information. A special interactive "products" map allows visitors to see what products are available in their area.

What's New provides a new recipe every day and also presents the most up-to-date issue of Food Forum, a quarterly publication by Kikkoman which examines a broad range of food-related topics.

The Bulletin Board features a FAQ (frequently asked questions) page and a Readers Voice which provides e-mail access as well as an Add Your Own Recipe page where visitors can contribute their own creative recipes, some of which Kikkoman may add to the Cookbook.

> *The Cookbook* contains 50 different recipes categorized by course. It allows visitors to select recipes according to their needs and preferred types of food. New recipes are added every month and old ones are stored in a comprehensive database.
>
> A special *Glossary* page within the Cookbook contains explanations of Japanese foods, ingredients, and cooking methods complete with photos.

"The recipe and cookbook are our fundamental marketing tools," said Masaki Miki, president of Kikkoman International, Inc., Kikkoman's San Francisco-based sales and marketing subsidiary founded in 1957. "We are selling culture, after all. We test what recipes go well with soy sauce and use them to introduce our products to new consumers. Our recipes introduce ways of using our products in various types of cuisines—namely French, English, Italian, American, Mexican, Asian, tropical, etc."

According to Kazuo Takei, senior vice president and national sales manager for KII, Kikkoman research has found that the average American family prefers six or seven different items for meals and simply rotates them day by day.

"So we create recipes for the most popular dishes, such as chicken, that use soy sauce," Takei said.

Soy sauce has been the perfect product for the 1990s, added Miki, who joined Kikkoman in 1959 after graduating with a law degree from Tokyo's Waseda University. Why? Because the trend has been toward lighter, less heavily seasoned foods rather than rich or oily dishes that are doused with seasoning.

"Kikkoman positioned itself as a premium brand…and then used soy sauce as a base to develop new products like stir-fry sauce, sweet and sour sauce, and teriyaki sauce for the U.S. market," added Miki, who is also a member of Kikkoman's board of directors.

Indeed, so popular has Kikkoman's teriyaki sauce become in the United States that it is already equal to about 80 percent of the company's U.S. retail soy sauce sales,

Yuzaburo Mogi pointed out in his message to stockholders in the company's 1996 annual report.

"I really admire my predecessors at KII," continued Miki. "They had the very ambitious strategy of selling the traditional Japanese flavor of soy sauce to Americans. By putting the words "all-purpose seasoning" on the label in the 1950s, Kikkoman moved soy sauce from the realm of a strictly Oriental condiment to an international seasoning. It wasn't easy, but they did it." While it may have been difficult, it's been a successful strategy. KII's North American sales have grown more than 30 times in the past 30 years for all 20 products Kikkoman sells in the United States.

One idea has been to expand sales by working with big restaurant chains and popular fast-food organizations. For example, Kikkoman sells powdered dehydrated soy sauce to a spice supplier that in turn provides ingredients for a leading hamburger chain's chicken snack. It also sells soy sauce to another supplier that makes a sauce for yet another popular family restaurant chain.

Food processors are another growing market for Kikkoman, according to both Miki and Takei. Kikkoman products are found in stir-fry vegetables, meat and poultry entrees, beef jerky, barbecue and other sauces, salad dressings, and even as a cure for bacon, sausage, and ham.

"One frozen foods manufacturer uses Kikkoman sauces in its products, and a frozen chicken packer includes Kikkoman Soy Sauce packets and Kikkoman stir-fry sauce," said Takei. "Another major food processor makes its own brand of teriyaki sauce with Kikkoman Soy Sauce as a base, and a popular barbecue sauce manufacturer also includes Kikkoman Soy Sauce."

Much of Kikkoman's recent success with American food processors is leading to an increasing amount of "cobranding" in which one company's logo is carried on the package of another company's product. For example, the Kikkoman logo can be found on the front of Birds Eye Easy Recipe Teriyaki Stir-Fry Meal Starter, an indication that Kikkoman produces at least a portion of the stir-fry sauce inside.

"We have reached promotion agreements with many manufacturers that allow them to show that our products are utilized as a seasoning ingredient," Miki said. "It's a phenomenon that endorses Kikkoman's application as a vital source [for their products]."

It's not part of Kikkoman's marketing strategy, Miki points out, but during 1996 and 1997, Kikkoman received an increasing number of cobranding requests from U.S. customers.

However, that's not the case with Kikkoman's World Wide Web home page, which is already becoming a strong marketing tool with "point and click" descriptions of all Kikkoman products and their uses. Even though Kikkoman's home page represents a significant technological step for the world's largest soy sauce maker in its journey from the feudalism of seventeenth-century Japan to the autonomy of twentieth-century cyberspace, Mogi and Kikkoman executives such as Miki and Takei see it for what it is: a new and potentially powerful marketing tool. The World Wide Web is not going to make or break Kikkoman. But in a world united by information technology as never before, it will certainly help put Kikkoman's vast array of foods, condiments, and biotechnology products before more potential customers than Mogi's ancestors could ever have dreamed of.

Nevertheless, when all is said and done, it won't be the marketing hype, the World Wide Web, the TV commercials, or even speeches before the World Economic Forum in Davos, Switzerland, that will propel Kikkoman into the twenty-first century. It will be leadership, a deep understanding of how the world works, and an ability to communicate honestly with employees and consumers alike.

"Yuzaburo Mogi is both a romanticist and an international humanist—a man who truly loves people," said Hiroo Takahashi, director of research at the Business Research Institute, a Tokyo think tank.

In addition to his business affiliations, Mogi also serves on the board of the International Youth Foundation and as a trustee of his alma mater, Columbia University. On top of that, he also serves as Wisconsin's honorary ambassador to Japan and as chairman of the Japan Soy Sauce Brewers' Association.

During the 34th annual conference of the U.S.-Japan Business Council held in 1997 in San Francisco, Mogi cochaired with W. Wayne Booker, vice chairman of Ford Motor Co., a critical discussion covering the issues of deregulation and market access, economic fundamentals and currency exchange rates, and the role of the United States and Japan in Asia. Those attending the conference were some of America's most powerful business leaders—people like Thomas Evans of Tenneco, Michael H. Jordan of Westinghouse Electric Corp., William Franklin of Weyerhauser Asia Ltd., and Robert E. Allen of AT&T.

"You have to love people in order to communicate naturally with human beings from all over the world, and Mogi is a natural communicator," Takahashi said.

In several domestic and international seminars, symposiums, and speeches between 1994 and 1997, Mogi demonstrated that Takahashi wasn't off-base in his assessment. Far from being a sedulous champion of Japanese business practices and government regulation, Mogi has consistently called for deregulation of the Japanese economy and changes in Japanese management style. For example, Mogi told one audience of young Japanese businesspeople that contrary to all the hype about Japanese management that saturated the media during the 1980s, Japanese companies were actually losing their dynamism.

"During the period of high economic growth [from the 1960s to the mid-1970s], Japanese companies had a strong incentive to move forward," Mogi said. "However, [in the 1990s] many Japanese businesspeople have become more administrative-oriented and less willing to take risks. In other words, the Japanese seem to have lost their entrepreneurial spirit."

The way to regenerate that spirit, Mogi went on, is for Japan to seriously promote and push deregulation of the Japanese economy. Creating a freer market environment in Japan will help Japanese people develop a stronger sense of self-responsibility, one that relies less on government regulation and protection and more on individual initiative.

Finally, Mogi said, Japanese companies need to create internal reward systems designed to provide incentives for innovation and the creation of new businesses. One way to do this, in addition to merit raises and other financial rewards, Mogi said, would be to create a "dual track" personnel management formula in Japanese companies that would replace the traditional "lifetime employment" system that currently prevails in most Japanese companies. One track would be for employees who work many years for a company, while the second track would be for employees who move from one company to another, taking advantage of their special skill sets, Mogi said.

Why have two? Because, said Mogi, there are some advantages of Japan's lifetime employment system that should be kept.

Lifetime employment, which essentially guarantees an individual a job for life, also "generates strong loyalty toward the company," Mogi said. "Loyalty to the organization and the terms of an employee's employment have a correlation, not only in Japan, but in any country. As employees work for a company for many years, gradually their loyalty to the company is enhanced. They can plan their lives and lifestyle accordingly, and that creates a sense of stability and loyalty among employees."

Japan's lifetime employment system also offers another advantage: excellent in-company education. Japanese companies like Kikkoman invest a lot of money in the training of employees because they expect them to work for the company for many years, Mogi said. They would never make that investment in employees who they know are planning to jump from one company to another.

To make a dual track employment system work, Japan needs to foster a labor market that facilitates the mobility of people from one company to another. To do this, a nationwide training program outside of Japanese companies should be created for people who change companies. After all, he continued, companies cannot be expected to invest money in the training of employees who may leave after a year or two.

The so-called lifetime employment system is just one of the four fundamental buttresses of Japanese-style management, Mogi said. In addition there is the *Ringi* system, the seniority system, and the company union. Ringi, or *Ringi Sho,* is a bottom-up system of decision making that seems to have evolved in postwar Japan. In most large Japanese companies, many proposals and ideas are often initiated at the lower levels of the corporation.

"It may be a section manager or even a lower staff member who begins the process," Mogi said. "The proposer, regardless of whom he or she might be, writes the proposal on a piece of paper called a Ringi Sho. Then the proposer takes the Ringi Sho to his immediate boss. If his immediate boss has his own opinions, then the proposal might be amended, reflecting his or her opinions."

No matter what opinions the boss may have, the Ringi Sho continues on its upward path in the organization. The proposer's boss passes it on to his boss and if his boss has opinions, they too are added to the Ringi Sho and passed on up the ladder to the next boss. However, the Ringi Sho also moves horizontally. For example, the proposer passes the proposal on to a related section or department where, once again, opinions and ideas are added to reflect the opinions of that section or department.

Some may wonder if, in all this vertical and horizontal movement, the originator of the idea might be forgotten. That's unlikely because the person who originates a proposal as well as each person who handles or amends it affixes his or her personal seal, or *hanko,* to the Ringi Sho thereby providing a kind of audit trail.

At some point, Mogi said, the Ringi Sho will make it to the board room where it is once again circulated among board members. Each board member who agrees with the idea puts his or her hanko on the proposal, and ultimately, the chairman of the board will circle the decision that has been made: approved, not approved, or pending.

This whole process takes time—much more time than it might take in an American corporation, Mogi adds. But once a decision is made, implementation is not only quick, but almost always is broadly supported throughout the company because just about everybody has had a chance to contribute opinions and ideas to the original proposal. In other words, those at the bottom levels of a company don't feel they are simply pawns in a chess game played by powerful senior managers. But even more important, the Ringi Sho system has allowed them to become familiar with the proposal as it has moved vertically and horizontally through the company. As a result, they feel reasonably confident that the proposal will actually be of some benefit and is not simply the by-product of some senior manager's ego trip.

All too often in American companies, an idea may rocket down the food chain from the top, but before it can be implemented, it is often sabotaged, subverted, or altered. As a result, the idea sputters and sometimes dies before it has a chance to have any impact. If an idea from the top is implemented, it often takes much longer to get things running smoothly than it does in a Japanese company which has spent much more time amending and passing a Ringi Sho throughout the organization. Once the go-ahead is given, it's with the knowledge that all concerns have been aired and all changes have been made to an idea *before* it is implemented.

But as good as the Ringi Sho system is, it also has its drawbacks, Mogi points out.

"It takes a lot of time to reach a decision," Mogi said. "When the proposal moves horizontally and vertically, a lot of time is consumed."

This is especially irksome in American subsidiaries of Japanese companies where American managers may feel the need to act quickly on an idea, but can't because the idea often must be circulated throughout the company's headquarters back in Japan.

"Another problem with the Ringi Sho system is that it might become a product or even a victim of compromise," Mogi said.

In the process of asking opinions from many different people in order to incorporate their ideas into the proposal, there may be a necessity to reach significant compromises. That means the idea may lose its sharpness or focus and may, in fact, wind up diluted or disjointed.

"For example, in designing a restaurant, we might use Mr. A's idea for the color of the chairs, Ms. B's opinion for the color of the tables, and Mr. C's ideas about the color of the walls," Mogi said. "Even though each decision by itself may be correct, the combination could turn out to be simply awful with colors that don't match."

As effective as it has been, Japan's bottom-up Ringi Sho system is being substituted more and more often by top-down decision making. The Ringi Sho system is still technically used because a president or senior manager may circulate his or her idea throughout the company, but in most cases, this is only a formality, Mogi says.

"In cases like these, the Ringi Sho loses its meaning," Mogi said.

But some Japanese companies—especially those that are in head-to-head global competition like Kikkoman—are finding themselves forced to implement decisions faster than the traditional Ringi Sho system will allow. That means a less traditional form of Ringi Sho—one that gives greater weight to the origin of an idea if it comes from the top and less importance to those people further down the corporate ladder who might want to alter it. As with other changes in Japan's management system, it is a result of increasing domestic and international competition.

"During a period of high growth, more lower level employees were willing to participate in these Ringi Sho decisions," Mogi said. "But under a more severe business climate, the number of decisions that have ended in failure has increased. Younger or lower level employees have become increasingly reluctant to initiate an idea or to participate in decision making in this kind of a climate."

Many employees have lost their confidence, especially if they already have been associated with one or more ideas that were rejected, Mogi suggests.

Yet another facet of Japanese management undergoing greater scrutiny and change at companies like Kikkoman is the deeply embedded seniority system.

"But despite the changes, age and terms of employment are important factors for wage increases and promotions in Japan," Mogi said. "In the United States, an employee's performance is evaluated once or twice a year, and as a result of these evaluations, promotions and wage increases are given."

While promotion and wage increases that are awarded because of a person's performance seem like a fairer system to Americans, in Japan, which is much less confrontational, the idea of merit raises and promotions is still not widely accepted. Why? For one thing, says Mogi, Japan's seniority system is more easily understood by employees and is much easier for managers and the human resources department to handle.

"If Mr. A. asks his boss why he has not been promoted to manager yet, his boss can say, `You know that it is still 3 years too early for you to become a manager,'" Mogi said. "This is a simple explanation and an employee cannot argue with it because age and terms of employment are a clear factor which can be understood by anyone."

Another component of the seniority system that is highly cherished by the Japanese is the kind of environment it engenders within even the largest corporations.

"It creates a kind of family atmosphere...and as in a family, people understand where they are within its structure," Mogi said.

For example, in a family, a younger brother comes to count on his older brother, says Mogi. At the same time, the older brother takes care of his younger brother, teaching him and guiding him. It's the same in a Japanese corporation. Younger or newer employees know their position in relation to older or more veteran employees. There is much less backstabbing and office politics than you might find in American companies because younger employees—no matter how ambitious they may be—are on a kind of predetermined "tenure" track. They realize that no matter what happens they will have to wait their turn for promotion. That allows them to concentrate on their work, rather than spending valuable time hatching plots to undermine a superior or a colleague. Unfortunately, while the seniority system may foster harmony, it does so at the expense of innovation and creativity, says Mogi.

"Highly motivated and talented employees who want to work harder, be promoted, earn more money, and become distinguished in their field have no incentives," Mogi said. "Even though they work hard and may be more talented than fellow employees, they cannot expect faster promotions or larger wage increases. They eventually lose energy and interest in their work, and in some cases, their performance may fall below that of less talented employees."

It is a scenario that, until recently, many Japanese companies have been willing to tolerate because internal harmony was more important than the need for innovation. But as the Japanese economy hit the skids in the 1990s, the kind of growth in Japanese companies that could sustain a harmonious seniority system stopped, Mogi said. Japanese companies could no longer hire large numbers of new employees. That not only meant fewer opportunities for promotions, but that companies would have to select employees for promotion or wage increases at an earlier age.

"There are those who say Japanese companies should lay off their employees during recessions or in hard times," Mogi said. "If we did this, they say, we would compete with American and European companies on a more level playing field.

"I do not agree with the drastic layoffs we see in America," Mogi said. "A stable employment system has been critical in Japan. It has generated loyalty between companies and employees, and I think this is a major factor in the strength of the Japanese economy."

However, Mogi added that the Japanese system should be changed in the megacompetition age. Japanese companies have to develop their own system of "soft" or moderate layoffs.

Another catalyst in Japan's rapid economic rise after World War II has been the company or enterprise union, Mogi adds. It's a unique system that evolved during the U.S. occupation of Japan from 1945 to 1952. Japan's unions—severely controlled during Japan's imperial government days—were essentially resuscitated by labor associations that the occupation allowed to thrive. Today, more than 90 percent of Japan's 12 million union members belong to some 33,000 different company unions, according to the Japan Institute for Social and Economic Affairs.

Instead of different employees belonging to different unions, as is often the case in American companies, Japanese employees—no matter what their jobs—belong to a single company union. A company union may have a membership consisting of a broad range of the company's workers—from truck drivers, clerks, and sales staff to factory and maintenance workers. Each plant has its own union association which negotiates locally on some issues and which may join with similar associations in the company's other plants to represent a company's work force nationally. But because it is a company union and not a national union, it is easier for union leaders and management to find common objectives, Mogi says.

"The union understands that in order to get more, the company has to gain more," Mogi said.

It understands this because its negotiators are also employees of the company. As such, they have an intimate knowledge of the company, its policies, and its management team.

"In the United States, union leaders do not have such common interests with management," Mogi said. "Their interests are simply to get more from management for the union members."

Perhaps the biggest difference between Japanese-style management and American-style management is found in approach, says Mogi.

"Japanese-style management attaches great importance to human factors, whereas American-style management seeks efficiency," Mogi said. "In the United States, there are some opinions that Japanese-style management was the main reason for Japan's high economic growth in the past." This might be true to some degree, but there may be another explanation, adds Mogi. It may be that Japanese-style "humanitarian" management, which is sometimes less efficient than its more cold-blooded American counterpart, was able to survive and thrive *because* of Japan's high economic growth from the 1950s to the mid-1970s—not the other way around.

In other words, Mogi suggests, there may have been some unique factors in postwar Japan that allowed Japanese companies like Kikkoman to adopt the lifetime employment system, the Ringi system, the seniority system, and the company union. For example, the close cooperation between Japan's bureaucracy, its manufacturers, and its financial sectors during the past five decades may have acted as a kind of benign "breeding ground" for a system of management that is peculiar to the Japanese business environment.

Attempts to transfer this system of management to American companies have not always met with success. In fact, stories of how American companies failed in these efforts are almost as numerous as stories of those companies that have failed in their struggle to reengineer themselves. Nevertheless, says Mogi, the philosophy behind Japanese-style management appears to be universal and, therefore, transferable.

"The main philosophy behind the Japanese system is respect for people," Mogi said. "Of course, there are companies in America, Europe, and other places that also have this philosophy, but I feel it can be found more often in Japanese companies than in companies outside of Japan."

When Kikkoman set up its first U.S. manufacturing facility in Walworth, Wisconsin, in 1972, it didn't intend to export its management system. In fact, Kikkoman's intention was to manage its 600 American employees the "American way," Mogi points out.

"But without intending to do it, we have taken the philosophy behind Japanese-style management to our operations in the United States," Mogi said.

In some cases, pieces of the philosophy have been used where appropriate, and for the most part, they have fit in successfully with the American work force. While Kikkoman has not exported its seniority system to its U.S. operations, it nevertheless places more emphasis on issues of seniority and loyalty when it evaluates American workers once or twice a year, says Mogi.

And even though Kikkoman has not taken its Ringi Sho system of decision making to the United States, it nevertheless makes more group decisions than most American companies do. Sometimes it could be frustrating, recalls Bill Wenger, retired manager of the bottling and warehouse department in Kikkoman's Walworth plant.

"The biggest problem I had was adjusting to Kikkoman's way of making decisions by consensus," said Wenger, a former U.S. marine who went to work in Kikkoman's Walworth plant just after it started operations in 1973.

"It seemed like it took forever for them to decide something, but when they finally agreed on something, everyone would get behind it and make it work," he continued. "I learned to work that way."

Wenger also learned something else during some 25 years with Kikkoman.

"The Walworth plant is more productive than all of Kikkoman's other plants," he said. "One reason, of course, is that Walworth is more automated than most of the plants in Japan and other places. But another reason is because we were able to blend American and Japanese ideas of management."

Wenger also knows what Yuzaburo Mogi means when he talks about the "human factor" of management.

"When my mother died in late December 1994, Mr. Mogi sent a mailgram of condolence," Wenger said. "How many American CEOs would do that for an employee on the factory floor? It's such a small gesture, but it says so much about Kikkoman and the Mogi family."

Another example of Kikkoman practicing what Mogi preaches about the human factor could be found in the way Japanese managers talked to their American workers.

"They would say, `Would you please do this or that?'" Wenger said. "They were always polite. No yelling or foul language. And it wasn't just for show. They made you feel wanted. At Kikkoman, you weren't just some number; you were somebody. I'll never forget that. It was the best place I ever worked."

Kikkoman basically follows the U.S. management methods in the United States but uses the Japanese philosophy of maintaining jobs during difficult times. While giving lip service to the Japanese system, American companies still resist many of the more human or "soft" management policies that have come out of Japan in recent years. But even in Japan, which has achieved enormous success using its uniquely human management style, things can stand some improvement.

As Japan's businesses restructure, Mogi told an audience of the Young Presidents Organization in Yokohama in 1994 that the Japanese government needs to provide a more favorable atmosphere for foreign investment. At the same time, Japanese companies should try to invest more in the United States and elsewhere rather than relying on exports from Japan. To many in the audience, these seemed like radical ideas, coming as they were from the leader of one of Japan's oldest companies. But anybody who has followed Yuzaburo Mogi's career at Kikkoman should not have been surprised by them.

Indeed, in another speech to the Japan Society in New York, Mogi tackled the issue of trade friction between the United States and Japan. He told his audience that the Japanese must admit that their markets are not as open as U.S. markets, though probably more open than many Americans may think. Nevertheless, as Japan heads into the twenty-first century, it needs to deregulate its markets more than they already are, he said. That will increase domestic demand, which in turn will reduce the need for Japanese companies to rely so heavily on exports.

But the Japanese people cannot depend on the Japanese government to do these things, Mogi said. There has to be some help from Japan's private sector. Mogi then offered an example. In Japan, he said, the Japan Chamber of Commerce and Industry and the American Chamber of Commerce in Japan created in 1986 something called the Japan-America Cooperative Committee (now Conference), or JACC, to deal at the private level with trade issues and other problems between Japan and the United States.

Mogi, who has served as cochairman of the JACC since 1994, along with the president of the American Chamber of Commerce in Japan wasted no time in tackling some significant pet peeves, including deregulation. For example, the JACC was able to persuade Japan's Ministry of Posts and Telecommunications to establish a bulk mail discount service. And it convinced the government and its regulatory agencies to relax rules for imported leisure boats as well as the use of wireless communications for oceangoing vessels. It also won a 20 percent discount for inbound free-dial telephone service, similar to America's "800" service, worked to get the Japanese government to relax regulations on additional bulk discount telephone charges, and pushed to establish new services such as Wide Area Telecommunications Service (WATS) to Japan. So what's all that got to do with Kikkoman and soy sauce? Everything, says Mogi.

"The Japanese economy is changing dramatically. In the past, so-called administrative guidance by the government worked well because the objective was to catch up with the United States and the rest of the world."

In the 1950s and 1960s, Japan's system of administrative guidance helped struggling, cash-poor Japanese companies enter foreign markets by providing everything from technical expertise to low-cost capital. Today, Japan has not only caught up with the West, but hundreds of Japanese companies are global leaders in their industries. Administrative guidance is an antiquated concept whose time has come and gone.

"Japan is a front runner today," Mogi said. "We no longer need the government to decide the allocation of resources. This must be decided by the market."

A free market system, said Mogi sitting in Kikkoman's Tokyo headquarters, demands a competitive, not a controlled, or guided, economy.

"It is time for the government to withdraw from the scene," he continued. "We need more free competition in Japan and we need more transparent business rules with a global standard. The government can monitor how corporations behave, and if they violate laws, it can penalize them. But it should not overregulate them or the Japanese economy."

Japanese companies like Kikkoman will have to enter the twenty-first century without government handholding, Mogi adds. They will have to be more innovative and creative than ever and they will have to be ready to take more risks than they ever have. This is especially critical as Kikkoman continues to globalize its operations.

It's all part of a broader ambition at Kikkoman—an ambition that you could say calls for spreading "Soy to the World."

Conclusion

Someone once said that you cannot discover new oceans unless you have the courage to lose sight of the shore. It's a great definition of risktaking. Losing sight of Japan's shore is something the Kikkoman Corporation has been doing for almost half of its 300-plus-years of existence. It began when members of the Mogi clan began shipping kegs of Kikkoman brand soy sauce to Hawaii and California in 1868—the same year Japan opened its doors to the world after almost 300 years of self-imposed isolation. And it didn't stop there. Kikkoman went on to set up a subsidiary in San Francisco in 1957 that has become a benchmark model of how to introduce a relatively unknown product (Japanese shoyu) to the mainstream U.S. market.

By 1973, Kikkoman's first U.S. soy sauce plant was up and running in Walworth, Wisconsin—the first substantial Japanese manufacturing presence ever in the United States. Setting up the Walworth facility was one of a handful of seminal events in Kikkoman's long history that have moved the company forward. It probably never would have happened if it hadn't been for the persistence and determination of Yuzaburo Mogi, a descendant of the company's founding Mogi family.

Like his father, Keizaburo, and a majority of his soy sauce producing ancestors, Yuzaburo Mogi is a consummate risktaker. But he is also a man who has a sense of where Kikkoman needs to go. Today, as president and CEO of Kikkoman, Mogi is still taking risks and is still guiding the Kikkoman ship toward new oceans.

In early 1997, Japan's oldest continuously operated enterprise broke ground for a new soy sauce plant in Folsom, California. In the fall of 1997, it opened a new plant in the Netherlands, bringing Kikkoman's overseas production facilities to five. And as this book went to press, the company was doing its due diligence with marketing surveys and other activities to prepare the way for possibly another new plant in China.

Taking risks has no doubt been a critical part of Kikkoman's success. But if Kikkoman's success was only a result of taking risks, one might assume the company had simply experienced an incredible run of luck. While luck may play a role in all human endeavors, it alone cannot explain Kikkoman's remarkable longevity or its extraordinary string of successes.

More than 2500 years ago, not long after the original forerunner of today's soy sauce was first created, some Taoist sages may have put their fingers on it: "Success is a matter of timing, not contention," they wrote, adding that lasting success seldom comes as a result of brute force, but rather as a result of good timing. "Successful people are economical in their actions and careful about time," they wrote in a classic collection of Taoist philosophy entitled *Huainanzi* (*The Masters of Huainan*) penned during China's Han Dynasty.

Kikkoman's success has no doubt been a result of good timing. But it has also been the result of some shrewd marketing decisions—not the least of which was the deft addition of two words on the Kikkoman label: "all-purpose." When they were added to the Kikkoman Soy Sauce label in the mid-1950s, it had the subtle effect of repositioning

Kikkoman Soy Sauce in the minds of the consumer. It was no longer just an Oriental soy sauce; it was an international "all-purpose seasoning."

At the time, it was considered an important thing to do. But today, marketing experts around the world point to it as a classic example of successful and distinct brand positioning. Some Kikkoman executives insist today that this one serendipitous move was the most crucial decision ever made by Kikkoman in its drive to enter international markets. It moved soy sauce from the realm of a strictly Oriental condiment that consumers only used when they wanted something to splash on their chow mein or chop suey in the local Chinese restaurant to a critical, yet subtle seasoning that they could use at home to enhance the flavor of everything from hamburgers, turkey, and pot roasts to salads, soups, and vegetables.

Today, soy sauce is found on the shelf of just about every supermarket in America. In many of the world's kitchens, soy sauce is no longer regarded as an exotic seasoning the way it often was in the early part of the twentieth century, but as a seasoning-condiment that's almost as familiar to consumers as pepper, ketchup, and mustard.

Unlike automobiles, electronic goods, steel, textiles, or any of dozens of other manufactured goods, naturally brewed Kikkoman Soy Sauce is such an original Japanese product that, when first exported to the United States, it was not a threat to anybody. For one thing, there was no indigenous naturally brewed soy sauce industry in the United States. There still isn't, though two Japanese competitors of Kikkoman have set up production facilities in Oregon and Virginia. Nor did thousands of Americans lose their jobs because of Japanese soy sauce imports. Today, 100 percent of Kikkoman Soy Sauce and probably 90 percent of all the other Kikkoman products Americans buy are made in the United States by American workers. In all, Kikkoman employs more than 600 Americans at its U.S. plants, offices, and distribution centers—almost one seventh of Kikkoman's 4300 or so worldwide employees.

At the same time, all of the raw materials used in Kikkoman's U.S. production (soybeans, wheat, salt, and water) are locally procured. Kikkoman also buys most of the machinery and production equipment locally. Only those highly specialized items unique to soy sauce production are bought in Japan.

While Kikkoman's localization policies regarding business and production are often applauded, the company also receives high praise for its genuine commitment to the communities it operates in. In the United States, for example, Kikkoman has been involved in everything from local 4-H projects to setting up college scholarships for high school students.

But localization policies and community involvement, while deeply ingrained in the corporate culture of Kikkoman, are nevertheless the means to an end. That end was first achieved in the spring of 1983 when Kikkoman bypassed La Choy and Chun King to become America's number one soy sauce manufacturer. By 1994, Kikkoman had about 50 percent of the market. Since 1983, Kikkoman has never once lost its number one position.

There is a reason for that, and all you have to do is look at the label of a soy sauce bottle to see it. La Choy and Chun King, Kikkoman's two main American competitors, produce nonbrewed or acid-hydrolyzed *chemical* soy sauce. It's a process in which soybeans are heat treated for 15 to 20 hours with hydrochloric acid. Then a laundry list of ingredients is added, including caramel coloring, corn syrup, water, and salt. The whole process is accomplished in a matter of hours, and the result is a chemically produced soy sauce that can be distinguished by its salty taste and opaque dark, almost black, color.

Kikkoman's soy sauce, meanwhile, is naturally fermented—a process that can take several months. Kikkoman's natural ingredients are water, wheat, soybeans, and salt. Even the most unknowing nose or palate can tell the difference between naturally brewed and acid-hydrolyzed soy sauce when the two are placed side by side.

As dominant as Kikkoman is when it comes to producing and marketing naturally brewed soy sauce, it is not stopping there. It is taking advantage of the fact that it is one of the world's oldest biotechnology companies. Naturally brewed soy sauce is, after all, one of the oldest—if not *the* oldest—biotech products in the world. Yuzaburo Mogi and other members of Kikkoman's strategy-creating brain trust have designated biotechnology and genetic engineering as a key growth area for the company as it enters the twenty-first century.

Not only is it continuing to expand production of biotech products for the global pharmaceutical, health, and food-processing industries, but it is also increasing research and development outlays in those areas as well. It is also pushing ahead with several new strategic products designed to make Kikkoman the number one producer and purveyor of Japanese food seasonings worldwide.

"Above all," Mogi says, "Kikkoman will strive to maintain the highest standards for our products and services and step up our efforts to raise the quality of people's lifestyles in communities around the world."

To accomplish these goals, Kikkoman has implemented what Yuzaburo Mogi characterizes as "a stronger, more flexible management structure" throughout the company. It's a structure that includes merit-based pay scales, incentives to reward innovation and creativity, and several other changes designed to make management more efficient and more responsive to the consumer. These are significant shifts for a traditional company with roots that go back to feudal Japan. But they are necessary if Kikkoman is to maintain its position as the largest producer of one of the world's oldest food products (soy sauce) while remaining on the cutting edge of biotechnology and genetic engineering.

As traditional a company as Kikkoman is, it is also a company with a rich history of risktaking. Under Yuzaburo Mogi's leadership, there is little doubt that it will continue into the next millennium.

There is an old Japanese homily that says: "A frog in the well does not know the ocean." (*I no naka no kawazu, taikai o shirazu.*) As this book demonstrates, Kikkoman decided long ago to leave the well. Kikkoman is a company that knows many oceans.

But as adventurous as Kikkoman is, it is also a company that understands the subtle message behind yet another Japanese axiom: *Isogaba maware.* Translation: "Make haste slowly."

INDEX

About the Author

Ronald E. Yates is an award-winning journalist, writer, and lecturer who worked more than 25 years as a foreign correspondent, national correspondent, and financial writer for the *Chicago Tribune*. He is currently a professor of journalism and head of the Department of Journalism at The University of Illinois, Urbana/Champaign. Yates' innate understanding and fascination with Japanese society and culture come from ten years of living in Japan, where he served twice as the Tokyo Bureau Chief for the *Tribune*. He is a nationally recognized authority on the global economy, American corporate competitiveness, international trade, and U.S. foreign relations.

Breinigsville, PA USA
13 April 2011
259736BV00002B/16/A

9 780071 347365